CONTENTS

KV-622-070

OUR CHANGING DEMOCRACY
Devolution to Scotland and Wales

*Presented to Parliament by the Lord President of the Council,
Secretary of State for Scotland and Secretary of State for
Wales by Command of Her Majesty
November 1975*

LONDON
HER MAJESTY'S STATIONERY OFFICE
95p net

Cmnd. 6348

If any readers of this White Paper wish to express views to the Government on the proposals it sets out, they may like to write to one of the addresses set out below.

Scottish Office
Room 2/16
New St Andrew's House
St James' Centre
Edinburgh EH1 3SX

Welsh Office
Room 40/G
Cathays Park
Cardiff CF1 3NQ

Northern Ireland Office
Room 8
Stormont Castle
Belfast BT4 3ST

Cabinet Office
Constitution Unit
Room 14/1
Great George Street
London SW1P 3AQ

PART I: INTRODUCTION

1. The fact that our democratic institutions have been admirably stable over a long period does not mean that they are perfect. A healthy democracy must develop and adapt itself to changing circumstances. The activities of central government now include substantial powers and functions that could be exercised at a level closer to the people. The case for this is especially strong in Scotland and Wales, where there is a keen sense of being Scottish or Welsh as well as British. This was the main reason for the decision announced by the Government in a White Paper* in September 1974 to set up in Scotland and Wales elected assemblies with wide responsibilities.

2. The 1974 decision was taken after extensive public discussion on a consultative document, and clearly met the aspirations of the majority of the Scots and the Welsh. That decision was however only the beginning. The constitutional changes proposed are the most fundamental of their kind in Great Britain for centuries, and raise complex and far-reaching problems. There are few parallels anywhere for dividing between two levels of government the powers and functions long exercised centrally in a unitary state. The new system must work efficiently as well as democratically, and it must stand the test of time.

3. The White Paper of September 1974 indicated in broad terms the roles and powers of the Assemblies and the subject areas in which they would operate. This White Paper turns those general principles of devolution into detailed proposals. It explains how the new institutions would work, what subject areas would be devolved, how continuing United Kingdom interests would be looked after, and how the financial principles outlined in the earlier White Paper would be implemented. The proposals rest on wide-ranging and intensive studies. The activities of every Government Department have been examined in detail to establish how devolution should affect them. The difficult economic problems relating to expenditure and taxation by devolved administrations have been thoroughly examined. The elements interact in complex ways, and great care has therefore been necessary to ensure that the final proposals form a consistent package.

4. In the Government's view the proposals set out in this White Paper are coherent and workable, and provide a sound basis for legislation. They envisage a massive handover to the new elected Assemblies of responsibility for the domestic affairs of Scotland and Wales, within the firm continuing framework of the United Kingdom. They will give closer democratic control

---

* Democracy and Devolution: **Proposals for Scotland and Wales (Cmnd 5732).**

and will help to foster the distinctive national traditions of Scotland and Wales, which are widely valued throughout the United Kingdom as part of our common heritage. They will give new scope for meeting the particular needs and desires of the people of Scotland and Wales. The United Kingdom has never been a monolithic state, and this fresh recognition of our diversity within it can reinforce our fundamental unity.

5. The Government recognise however that these proposals concern the whole of the United Kingdom. Two issues are of particular importance —achieving a sound and stable distribution of responsibilities between Westminster and the devolved administrations; and ensuring that the proposals meet the reasonable needs of Scotland and Wales, while maintaining a fair balance between their interests and those of the rest of the United Kingdom. The Government now want to see full public and Parliamentary consideration of the proposals. The issues are extremely important for all the people of the United Kingdom; the arrangements proposed are novel; and in constitutional matters, where frequent change would be harmful, there is a need for the widest possible basis of agreement on the essential features before legislation is enacted which will inevitably be very complicated. The main structure of the schemes is clear, but they need not represent the last word in every respect. The Government will therefore be very willing to listen to representations about their proposals that are consistent with the basic approach set out in Part II of this White Paper.

6. Work is in hand on drafting a Bill, which will take account progressively of points made during consultation. It will be published in the spring of 1976. It would not however be feasible then to carry so major a Bill through to Royal Assent in the 1975/76 session. Moreover, the Government believe that it would be wrong to legislate in haste on issues be very complicated. The main structure of the schemes is clear, but they published, will provide the opportunity for debate and for focussing opinion more closely on specific legislative proposals; and the Government will take account of all this in further refining the schemes. They will then introduce a Bill in Parliament at the start of the following session.

7. The unity of the United Kingdom does not mean uniform treatment for all its parts. This White Paper is about devolution to Scotland and Wales, and its proposals are related to their circumstances. As the White Paper of September 1974 made clear, Northern Ireland is in a different category. Its history and geography distinguish it from other parts of the United Kingdom, as does the presence of two separate communities. Its problems are not those of Scotland or Wales, and therefore do not necessarily require the same treatment. England is different again, and the Government will publish separately a document to provide a basis for discussion of possible future arrangements in England.

8. Part II of this White Paper outlines the Government's general approach to devolution. Part III sets out the scheme for Scotland and Part IV the scheme for Wales; to make each reasonably self-contained, there is

inevitably a good deal of repetition between them. Part V reviews the decentralised responsibilities of Scottish and Welsh Ministers in the United Kingdom Government—the Secretary of State for Scotland and the Lord Advocate, and the Secretary of State for Wales. Part VI deals with the cost of implementing devolution in Scotland and Wales. Part VII summarises the implications which the proposals for Scotland and Wales will have for the United Kingdom as a whole.

PART II: THE GOVERNMENT'S APPROACH

9. Political and economic unity has been maintained and deepened throughout Great Britain for over two and a half centuries, giving its countries a common history, heritage and way of life richer than any of them could have enjoyed on its own.

10. The Government are firmly committed to maintaining this unity. It is a powerful and constructive force shaping the daily lives of us all; and those who advocate destroying the United Kingdom, for the sake of a real or imaginary short-term gain to some, brush aside the long-term loss to all. The Government reject entirely the idea of separation for Scotland and Wales and the break-up of the United Kingdom, and believe that the vast majority of Scottish and Welsh people endorse this rejection. As the Government made clear in the White Paper of September 1974, they agree wholeheartedly with the Kilbrandon Commission* in rejecting also federalism within the United Kingdom.

11. Unity however is not uniformity. Within the United Kingdom Scotland and Wales have kept their own identities, with distinctive elements of tradition, culture and institutions. Respect for these diversities has strengthened the Union far more than an imposed conformity could have done.

12. This respect underlies the long tradition of decentralisation of Scottish government—that is, the practice whereby large areas of government work for Scotland are carried out not in London but in Edinburgh, under Ministers answerable to Parliament at Westminster but nevertheless distinctively Scottish. In 1964 the Government extended this system to Wales; and its scope in both countries has recently been widened by the transfer of new responsibilities in the industrial field to the two Secretaries of State.

13. Decentralisation remains a useful means of ensuring that administration in Scotland and Wales is founded on an understanding of the needs and wishes of these countries; the Government will continue to use it and indeed in some respects to extend it, as Part V explains.

14. The Government believe however that something more is needed—the creation of elected as well as administrative institutions distinctive to Scotland and Wales. This is what devolution means. There will be new democratic bodies, directly chosen by and answerable to the Scottish and Welsh people for very wide fields of government.

---

*Royal Commission on the Constitution 1969-73; Cmnd 5460 and 5460-1.

15. The central task on which the Government have concentrated in developing the devolution schemes is to define those areas of activity where decisions affect primarily people living in Scotland and Wales. It would plainly be wrong to devolve to the Scottish and Welsh Assemblies powers over activities which substantially affect people elsewhere, or the well-being of the United Kingdom generally. The need is to achieve balance—to reconcile unity and diversity in a stronger and better system, offering more achievement and satisfaction to the parts while improving the efficiency and stability of the whole. In working this out the Government have observed the principles which flow from acceptance of the essential unity of the United Kingdom. They have also kept in mind the need for a consistent and coherent pattern of government, which will be clear and understandable to the people who work in it and the public whom they serve. The objective throughout has been the long-term advantage of the people of Scotland and Wales within the United Kingdom.

16. Under the Government's proposals, the Assemblies will control policies and spending priorities over a very wide field, including for example most aspects of local government, health, personal social services, education, housing, physical planning, the environment and roads, and many aspects of transport. They will have a very large block grant from the Exchequer and some power to supplement it from local taxation, and they will have the fullest possible freedom to decide how the money should be spent among the services they control. The Scottish Assembly will also be able to make new laws or amend present ones in these matters, and it will be responsible for most aspects of the distinctive private and criminal law of Scotland.

17. All these powers will enable the new Scottish and Welsh administrations to bring far-reaching influence to bear on the whole physical and social environment of their countries. That influence, together with the huge spending power* which they will control, will enable them to have a very marked effect also on their economic environment.

18. The new powers will not however be conferred at the expense of the benefits which flow from the political and economic unity of the United Kingdom.

19. Political unity means that The Queen in Parliament, representing all the people, must remain sovereign over their affairs; and that the Government of the day must bear the main responsibility to Parliament for protecting and furthering the interests of all. In particular, the Government must be able to do whatever is needed for national security; they must conduct international relations, including those flowing from our membership of the European Community; and they must maintain the national framework of law and order, guaranteeing the basic rights of the citizen throughout the United Kingdom.

---

* In 1974–75 public expenditure on the services proposed for devolution was about £2,000 million in Scotland and £850 million in Wales.

20.   Economic unity plainly means that the Government must manage the nation's external economic relations—the balance of payments, the exchange rate, external assets and liabilities, and economic, trading and other arrangements with other countries. But the principle reaches much further. The Government must be able to manage demand in the economy as a whole—to control national taxation, total public expenditure and the supply of money and credit. The Government must be able to regulate the framework of trade, so as to maintain a fair competitive balance for industry and commerce everywhere. Within the wider common market which the European Community is developing we already enjoy a common market throughout the United Kingdom, and any new and artificial barriers within that long-established market could be seriously damaging. And the Government must also keep the task of devising national policies to benefit particular parts of the United Kingdom, and of distributing resources among them according to relative need. This last point is the cardinal fact about our whole system of allocating public expenditure. Resources are distributed not according to where they come from but according to where they are needed. This applies between geographical areas just as much as between individuals.

21.   People are less and less ready to tolerate extremes of wealth and poverty alongside one another in our society. Unplanned economic forces, changes in world demand and the discovery of new natural resources can bring fortune or misfortune to large areas, and over the centuries almost every part of the United Kingdom has experienced this ebb and flow. In recent times successive Governments have increasingly sought to reduce inequalities; the fact that Scotland and Wales are at present classified in their entirety as assisted areas is evidence of this. So, too, is the fact that under successive Governments Scotland and Wales have continued to benefit from levels of public expenditure per head significantly higher than the United Kingdom average. If these had been financed entirely by Scotland and Wales, their taxpayers would have had to pay much more.

22.   Regional policies have been formulated and implemented for Great Britain as a whole, so that priorities can be judged and the resources of the whole country deployed to help solve problems as they arise anywhere within it. Relative need can be assessed only by taking an overall view, and this must be the responsibility of the Government. It would not be practicable even to leave particular areas to draw up their own schemes of economic support and assistance within an overall allocation, since divergences could easily distort competition in ways incompatible with a unified economy.

23.   The Assemblies will have great economic influence, as paragraphs 16-17 above have explained. The Scottish administration will control the Highlands and Islands Development Board*. In addition, the arrangements for the Scottish and Welsh Development Agencies described in paragraphs 138 and 251 will give the Assemblies an important role in relation to the

---

* See paragraph 139.

work of these new bodies, which are intended to give a fresh stimulus to industrial and environmental regeneration. At the same time the transfer of manpower functions—crucial to economic development—to the Secretaries of State for Scotland and for Wales (paragraph 282) will add an important new dimension to the decision making in the economic field carried out in Scotland and Wales.

24. The complete schemes for Scotland and Wales are set out in Parts III and IV respectively. They are designed to give wide freedom to the new administrations in domestic matters whilst protecting the United Kingdom interest. But the Government do not envisage that after the new system is set up they and the administrations will deal with one another at arm's length. Every effort will be made in advance to cut out overlap and uncertainty, and to avoid the problems which ill-defined relationships would cause; but there will be many matters on which continuing close contacts will be in the common interest.

25. Arrangements will be needed for extensive but flexible consultation on many subjects and at all levels, political and official. Through these the Government and the devolved administrations will keep one another informed and will work together as closely as possible. Interests will sometimes differ, and give and take will be needed. But the Government see no reason to fear that the longstanding spirit of partnership within the United Kingdom will be lost; indeed, they believe that it will be enhanced. They look forward to working out effective two-way consultation arrangements with the devolved administrations as soon as possible, and to operating them constructively over the years.

26. At the same time the Government cannot shed their responsibility for the interests of the United Kingdom as a whole. They must ensure that they and their successors remain able to act freely and promptly in those interests. Reserve powers are therefore built into the devolution proposals to enable the Government of the day to intervene, subject to the approval of Parliament, in actions by the devolved administrations which the Government judge seriously harmful.

27. It is impossible to predict what situations might lead to the use of these powers, and it is largely for this reason that the Government propose to provide them rather than attempt to deal specifically in the Act with every possible eventuality. Their use should not therefore be regarded as a last resort implying a serious confrontation. But if the schemes of devolution fulfil their objectives, the necessity to use reserve powers should not arise frequently and need not be a source of conflict. The future of us all turns to a great extent upon harmonious co-operation between all the people of the United Kingdom and their elected representatives, whether in Parliament or in the Assemblies.

PART III: SCOTLAND

A. THE BACKGROUND TO DEVOLUTION

28. Ever since the voluntary union of Scotland and England in 1707 the arrangements for the government of Scotland have differed in some respects from those for England. In modern times these arrangements have centred on the office of the Secretary of State for Scotland. A Secretary for Scotland was created in 1885, but the present system dates effectively from the opening in 1939 of St Andrew's House in Edinburgh. It gives to the Secretary of State, who is a member of the Cabinet, a wide range of responsibilities for the administration of government in Scotland. These include most of the functions that in England are the responsibility of the Home Office, the Department of Education and Science, the Department of the Environment, the Ministry of Agriculture, Fisheries and Food and the health and personal social service sides of the Department of Health and Social Security, as well as (more recently) some functions of the Department of Industry. In addition, the Lord Advocate as a Scottish Minister has always had wide functions in the field of law.

29. This system gives Scotland a strong voice in the Cabinet and separate representation on interdepartmental committees where policy options are worked out. The Government intend that there should remain major roles for the Secretary of State and the Lord Advocate, as Part V of this White Paper shows. But the present system, based on Westminster with its wider burdens, cannot always be responsive enough to distinctively Scottish problems and characteristics. Factors like these have become more significant as the scope of government work and the calls on Parliament's time have grown.

30. The best way of improving matters in the particular circumstances of Scotland is by legislative and executive devolution. This means an elected Scottish Assembly which can determine its own priorities, pass its own laws and oversee the work of government. Scottish institutions and practices will be largely in the care of a purely Scottish body directly answerable to the Scottish people. It will be able, for example, to find more time than Westminister now can for Scottish legislation tailored to fit the distinctive law of Scotland and the separate legal system.

B. CONSTITUTIONAL ARRANGEMENTS

31. Many features of the constitutional scheme proposed are modelled on Parliament, where they are well tried and have evolved over the centuries in a practical blend of efficient government and democratic rights. Parliament must endow Scotland with a comparable blend. But the Government

do not intend that the new Assembly should be forced to be a carbon copy of Westminster. Within the main features which the Act must lay down and which only Parliament can change, the Scottish Assembly and the Executive answerable to it will be free to develop their own ways of working as they judge best.

The Scottish Assembly

32. There will be a single-chamber Scottish Assembly, initially with 142 members—two for each of the 71 Parliamentary constituencies in Scotland. There will not be time before the Assembly comes into being for the Boundary Commission for Scotland to complete the thorough scrutiny needed to divide the Parliamentary constituencies fairly. At the first election therefore each elector will be able to vote for two candidates, and in each Parliamentary constituency the two with most votes will become Assembly Members.

33. For later elections the Boundary Commission will divide Parliamentary constituencies as necessary into single-member Assembly constituencies, on a basis which will improve the fairness of the system by taking more account of the number of voters in each constituency. Each Parliamentary constituency will be allotted one, two or three Assembly seats, according to a formula based on the average size of Parliamentary electorates in Scotland. The formula will be this: —

a.	Parliamentary constituency whose electorate is less than 75% of the average electorate	1 Assembly constituency
b.	Parliamentary constituency whose electorate is not less than 75% and not more than 125% of the average electorate	2 Assembly constituencies
c.	Parliamentary constituency whose electorate is more than 125% of the average electorate	3 Assembly constituencies

On present electorates, this system would give an Assembly of about 138 members. The formula will be re-applied, and any necessary re-division made, whenever Parliamentary seats are redistributed. The divisions into Assembly constituencies will be embodied in draft Orders in Council laid before Parliament by the Secretary of State.

34. Everyone entitled to vote in Parliamentary elections, and also peers, will be able to vote in Assembly elections; but no one will have a vote in more than one constituency. The Secretary of State will be responsible for general oversight of Assembly elections and for making rules for them on election expenses and the like.

35. The Assembly will be elected for a normal fixed term of four years, but the Secretary of State will have power to make minor adjustments either way to give a convenient election day.

36. The time, place and other arrangements for the first meeting will be set by the Secretary of State. Thereafter these matters will be for the Assembly itself to decide.

37. Matters affecting Assembly membership, such as the rules about qualification, disqualification, expulsion and resignation, will be dealt with in the Act, as will the special safeguards which members will need to do their job effectively, such as protection against actions for defamation. Membership of the Assembly will not be barred to Members of the House of Commons or the House of Lords. Practical considerations will often prevent them from standing for election to the Assembly, but it does not seem right that they should be excluded by statute. Qualification and disqualification are dealt with in more detail in Appendix A.

38. Every candidate elected to the Assembly will have to swear or affirm allegiance to the Crown before taking his seat.

39. The pay and allowances of Assembly Members will be determined initially by the Secretary of State, and thereafter by the Assembly itself.

40. The Secretary of State will make interim Standing Orders to get the Assembly started, but thereafter it will make its own, subject to any requirements in the Act—for example on the use of committees (paragraphs 76-79 below).

41. The Assembly will elect from among its members a presiding officer, like the Speaker in the House of Commons. The Assembly staff will be answerable to the Assembly not to the Executive.

42. The Secretary of State will not be an *ex officio* member of the Assembly. But the Assembly and the Secretary of State could arrange by agreement for him to attend and address meetings from time to time.

The Scottish Executive

43. Executive powers in the devolved fields (including the power to make delegated legislation) will be exercised by a Scottish Executive. These powers will be vested in Members of the Executive, with each of them exercising whatever responsibilities are allocated by the head of the Executive—the Chief Executive.

44. The Executive will normally be formed after each election. The Secretary of State for Scotland will invite a prospective Chief Executive to form an Executive which will command the support of the Assembly; in the ordinary course he will invite the leader of the majority party. The prospective Chief Executive will submit the names of his proposed Executive to the Assembly, which will approve or reject them as a whole. If the Assembly approves, the Secretary of State for Scotland will formally appoint them as the Executive. If the Assembly rejects the proposed team, the Secretary of State will at his discretion invite the same person to try again, or someone else.

45.   The Secretary of State will also appoint Assistants to the Executive, on the recommendation of the Chief Executive. These Assistants will be political in character but will not be members of the Executive, nor require Assembly approval.

46.   Executive Members and Assistants will normally be members of the Assembly, but there will be no rigid rule about this. Some flexibility is desirable to leave room for possible appointments from outside the Assembly. It may be desirable to include a distinguished person, or one with special expertise (for example in the law), who is not an Assembly Member; and there will be no second chamber upon which to draw, as there is at Westminster. Political pressures should ensure that the scope for appointing non-members to the Executive is not over-used. The Assembly's right to approve or reject the Executive as a whole will be a strong factor.

47.   Executive Members and Assistants who are not Assembly members will be able to sit and speak in the Assembly, but not to vote.

48.   Maximum members of Executive Members, and of Members and Assistants combined, will be laid down in the Act. The Secretary of State will have power to increase the numbers later by Order. The pay and allowances of Executive Members and Assistants will be set initially by the Secretary of State and thereafter by the Assembly.

49.   Changes in the Executive (including dismissals) will be made formally by the Secretary of State on the recommendation of the Chief Executive; Assembly approval will not be required. If a Chief Executive misused his power of individual change to create a whole new team without Assembly approval, the Assembly could pass a vote of censure or no confidence. The members of the Executive will hold office formally at Her Majesty's pleasure, and the Secretary of State could in the last resort dismiss the Executive if he judged that it was holding on to office without commanding adequate support in the Assembly.

50.   Any departure of the Chief Executive from office will entail the resignation of the whole Executive and the Assistants. The Secretary of State will have power, without needing Assembly approval, to appoint a "caretaker" Executive to carry on business until a new Assembly-approved Executive can be appointed.

Scottish Assembly Legislation

51.   In subjects not devolved, Parliament will continue to make and control legislation for the whole of the United Kingdom. In devolved subjects however the Scottish Assembly will become responsible for legislation. At the outset the Executive will administer the law as it now stands; but the Assembly will be free to amend or repeal existing law and to pass new laws of its own.

52. As at Westminster there will be two kinds of legislation—primary legislation in the form of Scottish Assembly Acts, and secondary legislation in the form of Scottish statutory instruments. These statutory instruments may be made under the authority either of Assembly Acts or of Westminster Acts still applying to Scotland.

53. There will be no second chamber. Within the Assembly however the procedure for introducing and considering Bills will be very similar to that at Westminster. Having passed through all their stages in the Assembly, Bills will be submitted for Assent by Her Majesty in Council through the Secretary of State for Scotland. The following paragraphs set out the process leading up to Assent.

54. Either the Executive or individual Assembly Members will be able to introduce Bills (though if Bills introduced by individual Members entail expenditure they will be able to proceed only with the Executive's agreement). Any differences in handling will be for the Assembly itself to settle. The Act will lay down in broad terms various stages for the handling of legislation by the Assembly. There will be: —

   a. a general debate on each Bill, with an opportunity for Members to vote on its general principles;

   b. consideration of, and an opportunity for Members to vote on and amend, the details of the Bill;

   c. a final stage at which the Bill can be passed or rejected but not amended.

Further elaboration of the procedure will be left to the Assembly's own Standing Orders.

55. Some special procedure involving the Government will be needed for any Assembly Bill seeking to bind the Crown in respect of matters not devolved. The Government are considering what form this procedure should take, and at what stage of the Assembly's legislative process it should operate.

56. The Assembly's presiding officer, on the advice of his counsel, will report to the Assembly on the *vires* of a Bill (that is, whether it falls within the devolved powers) when it is introduced, and again before the final Assembly stage; if the report is adverse it will not stop the Bill but will serve as a warning to the Assembly and the Executive. The Government will not be formally involved at these stages, but they will be aware of the Bill and the presiding officer's report and may wish to give informal warning of any difficulties about *vires* which they foresee. The Scottish authorities will be similarly free, if in doubt, to consult the Government informally.

57. When a Bill has passed its final stage in the Assembly it will be forwarded to the Secretary of State. The Government will then consider, with advice from the Law Officers, whether any part of the Bill is *ultra vires*. In accordance with normal legal principles, ancillary provisions reasonably

incidental to a main purpose falling within a devolved field will be treated as *intra vires* even though they may not strictly relate wholly to devolved subjects. The Government will also consider whether the Bill is acceptable on general policy grounds.

58. In order to be submitted for Assent the Bill must be both *intra vires* and acceptable on policy grounds. If it contains *ultra vires* provisions, or is unacceptable on policy grounds, or both, the Secretary of State will send it back to the Assembly with a clear statement of the reasons.

59. It will be for the Assembly itself to decide how to handle any Bills referred back to it. If a Bill referred back as *ultra vires* is re-submitted to the Secretary of State in terms still adjudged to be *ultra vires,* he will tell the Assembly so and the Bill will not go forward for Assent. If a Bill referred back on policy grounds is re-submitted in terms which the Government are still not prepared to accept, they must within a set period from the Bill's receipt by the Secretary of State lay it before Parliament with a notice of motion praying for its rejection. If Parliament affirms this motion the Assembly will be told that the Bill will not be submitted for Assent. If Parliament rejects the motion the Bill will go forward.

60. The Government's reserve powers to halt the progress of Assembly Bills have necessarily been explained at some length. But this does not reflect the spirit in which the Government expect devolution to work, nor the features which will be most conspicuous in practical operation. In the ordinary course Assembly Bills will be presented for Assent without any trouble or delay.

61. Underlying all these arrangements there will remain the final legislative sovereignty of Parliament, in which all parts of the United Kingdom are represented. Parliament will remain able to pass laws on any matter and for any part of the United Kingdom. Any surrender of this sovereignty would imply federalism, not devolution. Against a background of co-operation and goodwill however Parliament would normally legislate on a devolved matter only where this was agreed with the Scottish administration* as being the convenient course.

62. The Scottish Assembly will be constitutionally subordinate to Parliament. It will have been created by Parliament and will always remain subject to Parliament's laws, and it will not be free to change the devolution settlement. The Government intend however that the Scottish Assembly should effectively assume, in the devolved field, the task of making laws for Scotland. Bills of the Scottish Assembly will be scrutinised, as explained in paragraphs 56-57, to see whether they are within the devolved powers. The question arises whether, after Assent has been given, an Assembly Act

---

* For convenience, here and elsewhere in the White Paper (except where the context clearly indicates otherwise) the term "administration" in relation to Scotland is used in a broad sense to cover both the Assembly and the Executive in their complementary roles.

should be open to review in the courts on the grounds of *vires*—that is, whether the courts should have jurisdiction to declare, at the instance of a litigant, that an Assembly Act goes outside the powers conferred by the devolution Act. The issue is more than just a legal technicality, and there are arguments both ways.

63. In favour of judicial review, it can be argued that this is a normal and natural accompaniment of the operation of a legislature whose powers are limited by law; that the right of the citizen to challenge in the courts any possible excessive use of power should not be abated; that the limits of what Parliament intended in the devolution Act should be subject to interpretation by the courts as specific situations arise in litigation, not merely by Government Ministers inevitably exposed to political pressures and making their judgments in the abstract before experience has been gained of how particular Assembly Acts will work in practical application; and that excluding judicial review will complicate the task of the courts, which will in any event have to take account of the devolution Act when they interpret Assembly Acts.

64. Against judicial review, it can be argued that its exclusion would have the merits of simplicity and finality and would therefore reduce doubt and room for argument, which might otherwise hamper good government, especially given the unavoidably complex division of responsibilities in the devolution scheme; that the Assembly will be taking over the normal practical responsibilities of Parliament, and the citizen should be able to rely on its laws as he now can on those of Parliament; that judicial review caused problems in the operation of the Government of Ireland Act 1920 and was therefore deliberately excluded by Parliament in enacting the Northern Ireland Constitution Act 1973; and that the three successive checks on *vires* before Assembly Bills become law (see paragraphs 56-57 above) should be a sufficient safeguard.

65. The Government would welcome public discussion before reaching a final decision.

66. There remains private legislation, promoted by private persons and bodies such as local authorities on particular matters which affect them but not the general public interest. In the devolved fields the Assembly should clearly have power to pass private as well as public legislation. But the procedures are complex, and it would be hard to fit the detail into the Act. The Government therefore envisage that the Act should contain a general provision enabling Her Majesty by Order in Council to provide for the handling of private legislation by the Assembly as soon as a suitable scheme has been worked out. If that has not been achieved by the time the Assembly takes over its main responsibilities, all Scottish private legislation, including that on devolved subjects, will continue meanwhile to be dealt with by Parliament. Present procedures already allow for hearings in Scotland.

14

Delegated Legislation

67. The Scottish Executive will be able to make delegated legislation under enabling powers contained either in Assembly Acts or in United Kingdom Acts still in force in the devolved fields.

68. It will be for the Assembly to decide what should go into its own Acts and what should be left to delegated legislation, and also to lay down any procedure required for delegated legislation under its Acts. Any procedure in the Scottish Assembly for delegated legislation under United Kingdom Acts will be required initially to correspond as closely as possible to whatever may be required in Parliament by the relevant Act; it is right that the Scottish Executive should at that stage be bound by the procedures for control of delegated legislation which were considered to be a necessary part of the Act when it was passed. The Assembly will later be free however, in the devolved fields, to pass Acts changing the procedures laid down in the original United Kingdom Act.

69. Where a United Kingdom Act in a devolved field lays down, in order to control expenditure, that delegated legislation shall be made jointly by two or more Ministers or with the consent of the Treasury or the Civil Service Department, the power will pass simply to the Scottish Executive. Where a United Kingdom Act confers a power exercisable by Order in Council, that power will be exercisable by Order of the Scottish Executive.

70. The Assembly will be required in general terms to make arrangements for the scrutiny of delegated legislation comparable to those operated at Westminster through the Joint Committee on Statutory Instruments. The Assembly will be able if it wishes to use its "subject" committees (paragraphs 76-79 below) for this purpose, or could set up a special committee.

United Kingdom Reserve Powers in Executive Matters

71. Paragraphs 56-60 above have explained the arrangements there will be to ensure that in primary legislation the Assembly does not exceed its powers or act in a way that would be seriously harmful. Some similar provision is required to cover other actions—that is, executive acts or omissions. (For this purpose the term "executive" includes delegated legislation.)

72. There is no point in devolving substantial powers and then maintaining detailed oversight from the centre. The Government could not monitor everything the Scottish administration do, nor indeed should they wish to. Nevertheless, the Government must have power to step in where necessary, either because matters not devolved—such as defence—are being prejudiced, or for wider reasons of their ultimate responsibility for all the people of the United Kingdom.

73. The Government will have to open them three methods, for use either separately or in combination: —

    a. for actions in prospect, whether involving a proposed subordinate instrument or some other proposed executive act, they will be able to issue a direction prohibiting the action or requiring a particular course of action (including the reversal of a previous action), subject to an affirmative resolution of Parliament within a specified period;

    b. for subordinate instruments already made, they will be able to make an annulment Order following an affirmative resolution of Parliament. In case of urgency the Order can be made without asking Parliament first, but subject to affirmative resolution within a specified period;

    c. for other actions already taken, or for omissions, the Government will be able, if the Scottish administration decline to put the matter right, to resume responsibility for the devolved subject in question to the minimum extent necessary—for the required place, task or period—with power to require and direct the use of the administration's staff and facilities for the purpose. They will do this by Order, subject to affirmative resolution of Parliament. The powers which the Government will be able to take by such an Order will be any powers available within statute law applying to Scotland, though any requirement for Assembly approval (for example by affirmative resolution on a particular sort of subordinate instrument) will be suspended.

74. As with the powers relating to Assembly Bills, these general procedures for intervening in the business of the Scottish administration are not intended for frequent use. They will be there in the background as reserve powers; and they permit wider devolution than would otherwise be possible. Their use will require the specific agreement of Parliament.

75. All this is about circumstances in which the Government need to intervene on grounds of policy as distinct from law. The legality of the administration's executive acts will be open to challenge in the courts just like that of the Government's own executive acts.

Assembly Committees

76. The Government believe it to be important for the success of the Assembly that all its Members should take a constructive part in the work devolved to the Scottish administration. The Assembly will therefore have a highly-developed system of committees to advise the Executive and investigate what it is doing.

77. There will be a committee of Assembly Members corresponding to each of the main subject fields of the Scottish Executive—education, health, and so on. The composition of these subject committees will broadly reflect the political balance of the Assembly as a whole; and they will be chaired by Assembly Members from outside the Executive. Their staff will answer to them and the Assembly, not to the Executive.

78. Before the introduction of major new policies or Bills, the Executive Member responsible will have to consult the relevant committee of the Assembly, except where the matter is especially urgent or confidential. Before a Bill is introduced the committee may discuss its principles and report on it to the Assembly, as a prelude to general consideration of the Bill in plenary session. The Assembly may remit the detailed examination of a Bill (equivalent to the Committee stage at Westminster) to the main appropriate subject committee with arrangements to associate any other committees whose subjects are affected. The committee may also scrutinise statutory instruments in its particular field. It will have the right to offer suggestions to the Executive, to initiate discussion and equities on particular topics, and in general to oversee the work of the corresponding Executive department.

79. Officials and documents of the Executive will be under the Executive's control; but committees of the Assembly will no doubt ask for Executive Members and their officials to give oral and written evidence, and it will be in the Executive's own interest to co-operate.

The Civil Service in Scotland

80. Members of the Executive will hold office under the Crown, and their officials will therefore be civil servants. The Government have considered whether these should constitute a separate Scottish civil service, or be part of the United Kingdom civil service. Most of them will in practice be people who are now United Kingdom civil servants in the Scottish Office.

81. The Kilbrandon Commission thought that there would have to be a separate civil service, on the grounds that a devolved administration would wish to choose its own senior officials, might not be content for general personnel matters to be handled by a Government Department, and would want to be able to rely on the undivided loyalty of their officials dealing with the Government, for example on the block grant.

82. There are however strong arguments for maintaining a unified service. It would help the consultation and co-operation on which the success of devolution will heavily depend. Present experience does not suggest that with a single service there need be divided loyalty; civil servants by tradition give wholehearted service to whichever Ministers are in charge of their Departments. We cannot assume that all staff will wish to transfer to a service entirely separate from that to which they were recruited, where the work, conditions and prospects might become substantially different.

83. Other factors must be taken into account. A separate service would need more staff (for example to handle personnel matters now dealt with centrally). A unified service would enable the Scottish Executive to draw its officials more easily from a wide pool of talent and experience. The wishes of the Scottish administration itself will be important, and these

17

cannot be known until it is in being. Finally, even if a separate Scottish service were desirable it could not be set up for some years; it is an option only for the longer term.

84. The Government believe that it will be in the best interests of all to keep a unified United Kingdom civil service. Any proposal for change would be a matter for discussion with the Scottish administration; staff representatives would be consulted at all stages. It would be essential to maintain the traditional independence of the recruitment system.

85. Numbers and costs of staff are dealt with in Part VI.

Complaints Machinery

86. Complaints against Government Departments can be investigated by the Parliamentary Commissioner for Administration, the "Ombudsman". Corresponding arrangements for the devolved subjects will need to be laid down in the Act. The details are outlined in Appendix B. The basic system for this important safeguard of the citizen's rights will be laid down by Parliament; but the new Scottish Commissioner will report to the Assembly.

European Community and Other International Aspects

87. The Government must remain responsible for all international relations, including those concerned with our membership of the European Community; no other course would be compatible with political unity. Every member state of the Community—including West Germany, for all its internal structure of federalism—is represented solely by its central government on the various bodies which deal with Community policy. It is the United Kingdom as a whole that is a member of the Community, and its Government must remain its sole spokesman, in the Community as in other international business.

88. Nevertheless, both in European Community and in other contexts international business touches increasingly on matters which will be devolved. The views of the Scottish administration on these matters, reflecting their own contacts with others concerned within Scotland such as local authorities, must be taken into account.

89. No formal statutory machinery is needed for consultation; it will be better to develop pragmatic arrangements between members and officials of the Scottish administration and the Government. These might operate most effectively through the Secretary of State for Scotland and through the particular Ministers representing the United Kingdom in Brussels or elsewhere.

90. There remains the question of how to ensure that any relevant international obligations are observed in the devolved fields in Scotland. There are two aspects to this: firstly ensuring that existing obligations are not breached, and secondly arranging that any positive action needed to fulfil new obligations is taken.

91. Breach of international obligation will be avoided in the normal way through the close consultation which the Government intend to maintain with the Scottish Executive. If, exceptionally, this does not work for any reason, and the Scottish Assembly sends forward a Bill or the Executive takes some action contrary to the United Kingdom's international obligations, the Government will be able to use their reserve powers for dealing with matters unacceptable on policy grounds. These powers have been explained in paragraphs 58-59 and 73 above. However, since international obligation is essentially a matter of fact and law (often involved and technical) rather than of general political judgment, the use of reserve powers in these cases will not require the approval of Parliament.

92. Ensuring that positive action is taken as needed to fulfil new European Community or other obligations is complex. On the one hand, the Government are answerable for getting this done. On the other, the Scottish administration, which will best know their own circumstances and legislation, ought not to be completely cut out of particular matters within devolved subjects whenever international commitments (including the increasing number of European Community ones) happen to touch on them. The best way of resolving this is for the Government to keep formal responsibility for all matters relating to international obligations, even when these matters arise in fields otherwise devolved; but for there to be power for the Government at their discretion to delegate to the Scottish administration, by Order, the job of taking any necessary action, whether legislative or executive, to implement the obligation. The power will be a flexible one, which can be used to delegate action either on a particular item, such as an individual European Community directive, or in a general field. The Government envisage that in practice it might well become the normal course to delegate implementation by agreement to the Scottish administration. The devolution Act will add the administration to the category of those who can be designated as implementing authorities under the European Communities Act 1972.

C. FINANCE AND TAXATION

93. Financial arrangements lie at the heart of any scheme. Those which the Government have chosen reflect their general approach to devolution, recognising continued political and economic unity and the need for close co-operation. Paragraphs 94-100 below explain the basic concepts, and paragraphs 101-113 set out their detailed application.

The Basic Concepts

94. The White Paper of September 1974 proposed that, as recommended by the Kilbrandon Commission, the financial allocation for the devolved services should be in the form of a block grant voted by Parliament, taking account both of local needs and of the desirability of some uniformity of standards and contributions in all parts of the United Kingdom; and that it should therefore be for the Assemblies to judge among competing claims.

95. Further study has confirmed that this is inescapable. Economic unity requires a system which considers the expenditure needs of the whole United Kingdom, including the claims of regions with special problems. This requires a decision each year on public expenditure for all parts of the United Kingdom by the Government, answerable to Parliament.

96. In theory one might base public expenditure for Scotland on revenues arising there. But even if they could be identified unequivocally, such a system would be quite incompatible with distribution according to need.

97. The Government are well aware that the discovery of major oilfields under the North Sea has given rise to ideas of a quite different kind. There are some who argue that oil revenues should be controlled directly by those parts of the United Kingdom off whose shores the oil is found, whatever the effect elsewhere. Let there be no misunderstanding: such a proposal—whether its advocates realise this or not—would mean the break-up of the United Kingdom. The Government believe that oil must be treated in the same way as other national resources (like the big coal deposits recently found in England, and the natural gas off its shores) and the benefits brought into the national pool for distribution in accordance with relative needs. Any other course could destroy not only economic unity but also political unity. Those who wish to reserve to Scotland oil or other revenues arising there are in effect demanding a separate Scottish state. The circle cannot be squared: it is not possible for Scotland—or any other part of the United Kingdom—to enjoy rights which can only go with separatism yet not to have separatism itself.

98. For their part, the Government rule out separatism. Even if on a narrow economic calculation Scotland might be better off materially for a time by keeping the benefits of oil exclusively to itself—and such a calculation would be at best highly precarious, resting on limited reserves of a single commodity whose value varies with the world market—the Government are convinced that the Scottish people are overwhelmingly opposed to destroying the Union. The Government repeat their pledge that all the parts of the United Kingdom most in need will receive their full and fair share of the benefits from the energy resources of the continental shelf, which belong to the United Kingdom as a whole.

99. The Government accordingly intend that Scottish public expenditure should be settled as part of the annual public expenditure review for the United Kingdom as a whole. The amount will be a matter for political judgment, on the basis of an assessment of relative needs made jointly with the Scottish administration through close and continuous collaboration. Once the relative amounts of public expenditure are established, Parliament will be asked to vote the appropriate element for the devolved services in the form of a block grant. In 1974-75 public expenditure on the services proposed for devolution was about £2,000 million, with a further sum of more than £100 million met by local authorities as loan charges. Had the proposed financial arrangements been in operation this would have involved

a block grant of more than £1,300 million, local authority taxation of £300 million and borrowing of about £500 million. Expenditure on the devolved services would have come to nearly three-fifths of total identifiable public expenditure in Scotland.

100. No neat formula could be devised to produce fair shares for Scotland (and for England, Wales and Northern Ireland) in varying circumstances from year to year. The task involves judgments of great complexity and political sensitivity. Nevertheless, objective information on standards and needs would help the Scottish administration, the Government and Parliament to make their judgments. Various arrangements might be adopted for collecting such information, and the Government will discuss possibilities with the Scottish administration.

The Block Grant

101. Once the block grant has been voted by Parliament, it will be paid over at regular intervals during the financial year. Accountability for the expenditure will run not to Parliament but to the Assemblies. The devolution Act must lay down certain basic features of the financial control system, but its running will be overseen by the Scottish Assembly.

102. The Scottish administration will have the fullest possible freedom to decide how the money from the block grant should be spent—how much, for example, should go on roads, houses, schools and hospitals, and where in Scotland it should be spent. As the figures in paragraph 99 demonstrate, this is a major economic as well as social power. It will give the administration a powerful new instrument for shaping developments over a wide range of services.

103. The Government's decision on the total amount for all the devolved services will not be a matter of simply imposing an arbitrary figure. It will be the outcome of a close and thorough process of consultation each year with the Scottish administration. Appendix C outlines how the process might run in a typical year.

104. The administration will base their proposals on their view of Scottish needs in the devolved fields. But the Government must take account also of other needs, both elsewhere in the United Kingdom and in non-devolved fields within Scotland. All these needs must then be related to what the United Kingdom can afford for public expenditure against other claims, including the balance of payments, private investment and private consumption, as well as the needs of public industries such as coal and steel which will continue to be very important to Scotland.

105. With understanding on both sides agreement should usually be reached on a total accepted as fair both to Scotland and to the rest of the United Kingdom. If agreement is not reached the matter will have to be settled by the Government, answerable to Parliament. Parliament, with its Scottish MPs alongside those from all other parts of the United Kingdom, is the right body to vote the amount for the devolved services, and to

settle the statutory limits on the administration's short-term borrowing and on issues to the Scottish Loans Fund.

Taxation

106. Scottish taxpayers will continue to pay United Kingdom taxes at United Kingdom rates, and these payments will contribute to the central pool of national resources from which the block grant and other national expenditure will be financed according to needs.

107. The Government have particularly considered whether the Scottish administration should be able to levy taxes. As already explained, there can be no question of sharing responsibility for taxation generally or of reserving for Scotland revenues raised there. The issue is rather whether the administration should have power to levy limited additional taxation, in order to finance extra expenditure which they think especially important. The burden would have to fall solely on Scottish taxpayers, as the people getting the benefits of the extra expenditure.

108. The people of Scotland may not want to pay more taxes regularly year after year in order to finance more public expenditure than the assessment of their needs in the United Kingdom context provides. Nevertheless, some powers for the devolved administrations to levy additional taxation would give them greater freedom. It is however difficult to identify suitable forms of tax. There is no point, for example, in choosing taxes unlikely to yield enough revenue to give much extra discretion; and it would be wrong to choose ones which would fall too narrowly on particular groups. Among the specific possibilities which have been considered, the two found to merit the most detailed study were a retail sales tax (distinct from VAT) and a surcharge on income tax. The studies showed that, for either of these, there would be great administrative complexities for both taxpayers and tax administrations; and also heavy costs, falling on retailers or employers as well as on the devolved administrations, for collection systems which would still need to be maintained and paid for whether or not any extra taxes were levied in a particular year. Both possibilities were therefore unsuited for use as supplementary taxes to be applied at a low rate and turned on and off from time to time. The Government have therefore concluded that the only tax power suitable for devolution is a general power to levy a surcharge on local authority taxation, whether on the rates as at present or on any new system introduced in the future (for example after the Committee of Inquiry into Local Government Finance— the Layfield Committee—has reported). No tax is popular, but a power of this kind would give the Scottish administration a useful degree of discretion. They will not have to use it unless they run into deficit or deliberately aim for a higher level of expenditure, for example to meet some particular Scottish priority for which they judge people would be willing to accept higher burdens.

109. Local authorities, who will run many of the devolved services, can settle their own levels of taxation, so that there will in any event be some flexibility in the total amount available for the services in Scotland.

The Scottish administration will decide both how much of the block grant should be distributed to local government and how to allocate it among individual authorities. In calculating block grant the Government will in general assume that Scottish local authorities will receive, in relation to their expenditure needs and their taxable resources, provision comparable with that for local authorities in England; whether they in fact levy more or less local tax, and are assigned more or less subsidy from the block grant, will be a matter to be settled in Scotland.

110. The sources of local authority taxation will be the same as in England. The Scottish Assembly will have legislative powers to adjust the application of the system of rating and valuation for rating to suit local conditions; but only Parliament will be able to authorise new forms of local taxation.

Other Sources of Finance

111. Capital expenditure by local authorities and by other public bodies in devolved fields will continue to be financed by borrowing. Local authorities will continue to have access to the Public Works Loan Board. Other public bodies will have access to a new Scottish Loans Fund for longer-term borrowing, financed from the National Loans Fund and controlled by the Scottish administration. The main condition on its use will be that on-lending should not be at a lower rate of interest than the corresponding loan from the National Loans Fund. The only long-term borrowing trans-actions controlled individually by the Government will be those involving foreign currency or overseas sources. However, the Government must also control both the total amount of long-term borrowing and within this the total of borrowing from official sources by local authorities and public corporations. These controls are essential for the management of the United Kingdom economy.

Financial Control and Audit

112. The Act will lay down certain basic features to ensure that there is a sound system for authorising expenditure and reporting on the accounts. In addition to the Scottish Loans Fund, there will be Scottish counterparts of the Consolidated Fund, the Comptroller and Auditor General and the Public Accounts Committee. The Assembly will have power to appropriate funds to individual services by Assembly Order, corresponding to Appropriation Acts at Westminster.

113. Responsibility for controlling issues from the Scottish Funds and for supervising the arrangements for monitoring and audit will rest squarely with Scottish bodies. The reports of the Scottish Comptroller and Auditor General will be presented to the Assembly and considered by the Scottish Accounts Committee, and it will be for the Assembly to decide whether to require comments or proposals from the Executive as a result. The Act will however require the publication of these reports, so that expenditure on devolved matters undergoes the same public scrutiny as the corresponding expenditure does now.

D. THE DEVOLVED SUBJECTS

The General Approach

114. It is important to recognise what legislative devolution will mean. Where a subject field is devolved, responsibility for the activities of government in that field will be transferred to the Scottish administration. Devolving a subject field in Scotland will not however be like transferring functions between Government Departments or between local authorities; it will mean much more. The present law will be inherited, but the administration will be free to change it. They will not be confined to the activities going on now. They could end these activities, or run them in different ways, or create quite new activities.

115. The Government intend to apply this far-reaching concept to a massive hand-over of responsibility for Scotland's affairs.

116. The Act will devolve certain subjects; anything not shown as devolved will remain the direct responsibility of the Government and Parliament as at present. The Government have in general approached the task of deciding which subjects to devolve from the positive standpoint of devolving wherever possible, and keeping subjects back (or making exceptions within subjects otherwise devolved) only where there is cogent reason for doing so—for example where devolution might risk damaging basic unity and the fundamental rights of United Kingdom citizenship, or where wider uniformity is plainly needed, or where devolving or dividing a subject would be very awkward to work.

117. Paragraphs 119-168 below set out the effect of applying this approach, and Appendix D gives a tabular summary. The Government believe that the result is well suited to the interests of Scotland and of the United Kingdom as a whole, and that the scale and character of the devolved responsibilities will enable the Scottish administration to take a broad and comprehensive view of their tasks in serving the people of Scotland.

118. The responsibilities to be transferred on devolution in the various fields will be those which the Government now carry. The proposals do not entail any removal of current tasks or powers from local government.

Local Government

119. Responsibility for central government supervision of most aspects of local government in Scotland will be devolved. The administration will oversee the work of local authorities in devolved matters, will allocate rate support grant to them, will control their capital investment in the devolved fields and will be responsible for the application of the local taxation system, as explained in paragraphs 109-110. The devolution Act will not change local government structure. The Government believe that it would not be in the interests of either the Assembly or Scottish local government for the new structure of local authorities and the distribution

24

of functions among them to be radically revised again in the next few years. These must however be matters in future for the Assembly; and it will be empowered to legislate on local government administrative and electoral boundaries, the detailed application of the rating system and the division of devolved functions between local authorities and the Scottish Executive, as well as on the structure of local government itself.

120. Responsibility will not be devolved for determining the qualifications for voting in local government elections; the qualifications and disqualifications for membership of local authorities; the voting system for local government elections; and the frequency with which they are held. These basic democratic features of the local government system should remain under the direct authority of Parliament.

121. The Scottish administration will not of course be responsible for any functions which Scottish local authorities continue to carry out in matters not devolved; the responsibilities of central and local government in these matters will not be changed by the Act.

Health
122. The Scottish administration will be responsible for health matters in Scotland, including the National Health Service. This means that they will be free to determine arrangements and priorities for the provision of health care, including the resources to be allocated. In this as in other fields (see paragraph 160 below), certain United Kingdom arrangements and standards will continue to apply—for example on medicines and drugs— but in general the administration will be able to vary the scope and character of current arrangements, and to decide policy on such matters as family planning, transplant surgery, abortion, private practice and the control of nursing homes.

Social Work
123. The Scottish administration will be responsible for the social work services, such as the care of children, the elderly, the handicapped and others in need of special care or support. They will be able to control the standards of private provision in these fields, and to make grants to voluntary bodies.

Social Security
124. The social security system, which provides a network of cash benefits payable to individuals and families, will not be devolved. It is necessary to keep a single system of cash benefits designed to maintain a decent minimum standard of living for every citizen throughout the United Kingdom. The war pensions scheme will also remain on a United Kingdom basis.

125. Some problems arise because of the close and often complicated interaction between social security benefits and schemes for rent and rate

rebates, rent allowances, and the minimum charges and personal allowances for those living in local authority homes. The Government's approval will be required for any changes in such schemes which would affect wholly or mainly people receiving supplementary benefits, or people who would receive them if the changes were made. The reason for this special provision is that the burden would then fall directly on United Kingdom funds, not the block grant or the rates. It is a more open question whether, because of the complexity of the interaction with social security generally, it would be better not to devolve powers relating to such schemes at all. The Government would welcome comments from bodies working in this field.

Education, Science and the Arts

126. The Scottish administration will be responsible for all educational and cultural matters other than those noted in paragraphs 127-129 below. They will control the schools system in Scotland, and will be able if they wish to determine (for example) its standards and structure, its curricula, its attendance requirements such as age levels, and policy for private schools and nursery education. They will be responsible for youth and community services and for all further and higher education except the universities.

127. Responsibility for the universities will not be devolved. The Government believe that it is in the best interests of the United Kingdom, including Scotland, that they should continue to be run as part of a wider United Kingdom system and under the supervision of a single University Grants Committee. At the same time, the Government attach importance to close and effective liaison between the Scottish universities and those other parts of the higher education system that will come under the control of the Scottish administration. The University Grants Committee will therefore be asked to devise arrangements recognising the specific Scottish dimension of their business, and linking the Scottish administration with these arrangements.

128. It would make no sense to break up the Research Councils*, and responsibility for them will not be devolved. The Scottish administration will be able (preferably in consultation with Government Departments concerned) to commission research from them. Responsibility for the Nature Conservancy Council will similarly not be devolved.

129. Partly because of the decisions explained in paragraphs 127-128, and partly also to avoid difficulties or friction in the present wide interchange of students among higher education establishments throughout the United Kingdom, responsibility will not be devolved for postgraduate awards and for awards to Scottish domiciled students on university and other courses of advanced further education (though the Scottish admini-

---

*The main civil ones are the Agricultural, Medical, Natural Environment, Science and Social Science Research Councils.

stration will be responsible for policy on awards made by education authorities to students following other courses of further education).

130. The administration will be responsible for the arts (except the export control of works of art) and for national and local libraries, museums and galleries.

Housing

131. The Scottish administration will be responsible for all aspects of housing, except that in order to maintain proper management of the United Kingdom economy the Government will remain responsible for housing finance in the private sector (building society mortgages and the like), and will also keep a reserve power to prevent or restrict increases in public and private sector rents where general economic and counter-inflationary policy makes this necessary. These limited qualifications apart, the Scottish administration will be able to have their own laws and policies, for both the public and the private sectors, on the provision and upkeep of accommodation, the control of rents, subsidies to local authorities and housing associations, renovation, building standards and slum clearance.

Physical Planning and the Environment

132. The Scottish administration will be generally responsible for physical planning and the environment. They will deal with the various aspects of land use—how to manage its development and control, how to co-ordinate land use planning with (for example) transport planning, and how to provide the general infrastructure needed for Scotland's prosperity. They will deal with the general improvement of the environment; the rehabilitation of derelict land; all aspects of water such as supply, amenity planning, arterial drainage, sewerage and sewage disposal; new towns; and the protection of countryside amenity and landscape.

133. The administration's powers over land must however be qualified. Firstly, it is essential that the new community land legislation should apply uniformly; divergences could lead to damaging economic distortions. The Scottish administration will however have substantial supervisory functions under the legislation. Secondly, the devolution of planning powers will be subject to a continuing right—which should not need to be used often—for the Government to "call in" any particular planning issue for their decision if the general United Kingdom interest is affected, for example on non-devolved matters like defence. The Government will probably also need to keep the right to settle any disputes over compulsory purchase affecting such matters.

134. The Scottish administration will be responsible for sport and recreation, parks and open spaces, ancient monuments and historic buildings, public and civic amenities, and a variety of other matters like refuse collection and disposal, cemeteries, markets, fairs and allotments. They will be responsible also for dealing with natural emergencies (though any use of the armed forces to help in these must of course remain a matter for the Government). They will be responsible for protecting the environ-

ment, including preventing nuisances, atmospheric pollution and noise, except that their powers will not extend to aircraft, motor vehicles and ships; some aspects of these are the subject of international agreements and others raise defence or other national considerations, so that they must remain matters for the Government.

Roads and Transport

135. The Scottish administration will be responsible for a wide range of transport matters. These will include the planning, construction and standards of roads; the application of traffic rules (except on motorways, where uniformity throughout Great Britain is important for safety); road safety publicity; local transport planning, including matters relating to passenger transport areas; road service licensing, including appointing Traffic Commissioners and deciding appeals arising from their decisions; bus and shipping services of the Scottish Transport Group; subsidies for shipping and air services to the Highlands and Islands, and for improving piers and boatslips; inland waterways; examining and paying claims for new bus grants; the current powers to pay fuel duty rebate to bus operators; and general oversight of local authority powers to subsidise passenger transport services, including rail and bus services.

136. There are certain matters in the field of road transport where, for safety reasons, practice needs to be the same throughout Great Britain. These include framing (as distinct from applying) rules for traffic management; motoring offences; the Highway Code; the system for testing and licensing drivers and public service vehicles; and the transport of dangerous substances. Responsibility for these will not be devolved.

137. Responsibility for local authority airports will be devolved from the outset. For airports owned and operated by the British Airports Authority the Government will discuss future arrangements with the Scottish administration, and aim to achieve a transfer of responsibility while retaining the managerial expertise of the Authority in Scotland. Similar arrangements would be made for aerodromes owned and operated by the Civil Aviation Authority.

Development and Industry

138. The Scottish Development Agency will have a key role in both the environmental field and the industrial field. The devolution Act will not change the powers of the Agency. Its environmental and factory building functions will be fully devolved, except that the terms of disposal of factories must remain under Government control—it would not be in the interests of any part of the United Kingdom to create the possibility of a price war in making industrial premises available to attract incoming firms. The other industrial functions of the Agency cannot be devolved, because of the need to preserve economic unity; the arrangements for dealing with these are set out in Part V, on the role of the Secretary of State for Scotland. Half the

members of the Board of the Agency will be appointed by the Scottish administration, which will also be consulted before the Secretary of State appoints the Chairman.

139.   For the Highlands and Islands Development Board, which deals with a range of specialised problems, responsibility for both economic and social activities will be devolved. The Scottish administration will appoint the Chairman and members, and in devolved fields such as tourism will have full discretion in supervising the Board's activities. But for Board activities in reserved fields, for example assistance to industry, fishing and agriculture, the Government will lay down a system of guidelines and cash limits on individual projects within which the Board and the Scottish administration will decide their own priorities; major industrial projects will be reserved to the Scottish Development Agency and the Secretary of State. Changes in the Board's powers and the geographical area which it covers will also be a matter for the Secretary of State.

140.   There can be no question of breaking up the main nationalised industries or splitting responsibility for them. The Government envisage however that there should be informal contacts between them and the Scottish administration on matters of joint interest, and that they should include in their reports information on recent developments and future plans for Scotland. The administration will be able to consider these reports, and to make representations to the industries or to Ministers.

141.   Relations with industry and commerce are an important element of managing the United Kingdom economy as a whole. Government Departments operating on a central basis will therefore keep their present statutory functions; but they will consult the Office of the Secretary of State or the Scottish administration on matters of common concern.

Natural Resources

142.   The Scottish administration will be responsible for functions relating to land and natural resources now carried out by the Department of Agriculture and Fisheries for Scotland. These will include crofting and freshwater fisheries, and also forestry functions—especially important in Scotland—with the exception (an essential consequence of United Kingdom unity) of fiscal, regulatory and international aspects. The Act will maintain the Forestry Commission, already based in Edinburgh, as the instrument for carrying out Scottish policies. For these it will be financed by and accountable to the Scottish administration.

143.   The administration will be responsible also for the management of agricultural estates now vested in the Secretary of State for Scotland, and for the improvement of fisheries harbours. The main aspects of agriculture and sea fisheries are however too bound up with overall United Kingdom economic management and international agreements for devolution to be practicable (see paragraph 280).

Law and the Legal System

144. The separate character of Scots law and of the Scottish legal system was specially recognised in the Union between Scotland and England, and in this distinctively Scottish field the Government believe that extensive devolution is particularly appropriate.

145. The Scottish administration will have wide responsibilities in the range of subjects constituting Scots private law, such as the law of persons, delict, contract, property, trusts and succession. The Government recognise the importance of the development and reform of Scots law as a coherent and distinctive system. There is however a complex interaction between those subjects and areas such as company law, industrial relations and consumer protection where consistency with the law in other parts of the United Kingdom is particularly important, for example in order to maintain a common framework for trade. Further study is proceeding to find the best way of reconciling maximum devolution in the field of private law with these wider United Kingdom interests.

146. The Scottish Law Commission will continue after devolution to have a major role in the coherent development of the whole of Scots law, whether in devolved or non-devolved matters. Because the Commission's functions will span both fields, legislative responsibility for its constitution and structure must remain with Parliament. The Scottish administration will however be responsible for appointing the Chairman and members of the Commission, for its running and for its general programme of work, though the Government will remain able to refer non-devolved matters to it.

147. The Scottish administration will also be given responsibility for the general criminal law, including the right to create new offences, to redefine or abolish existing offences, to determine penalties and to regulate the treatment of offenders (including prisons). There will however be certain exceptions. Firstly, there are those that may affect the security of the state, like the law on treason, espionage and measures against terrorism. Secondly, there are areas where the law can work efficiently only if it is uniform, such as explosives, firearms, and dangerous drugs and poisons. Finally, there are offences relating essentially to subject fields which will not be devolved, like taxation and road traffic law.

148. The enforcement of the criminal law through the police and the prosecution system—which in Scotland is not in any way under the control of the police—is part of the responsibility of the Government for the maintenance of law and order and the security of the state, and will extend to offences within both devolved and other fields. It would not be right that responsibility for law enforcement should rest with members of an administration not directly answerable to Parliament. The Secretary of State and the Lord Advocate will therefore retain their present responsibilities with regard to police and prosecution respectively. The police will retain their existing status and their relationship with local authorities, and the function of prosecution will continue to be exercised through the Crown Office and the procurator fiscal service.

149. The Government have considered with special care where responsibility should lie for the main Scottish courts—the supreme courts (the High Court of Justiciary and the Court of Session), the sheriff courts and the district courts. The Government are satisfied that responsibility for the different levels ought not to be split—separation would pose difficult problems over such matters as jurisdiction, procedure and administration. They believe that the supreme court judges should continue to be appointed by The Queen on the recommendation of the Government, and that responsibility for their tenure and conditions of office should not be devolved. The Government also believe that questions affecting the right of appeal from the Court of Session to the House of Lords—the court of final appeal in civil matters from the courts of every part of the United Kingdom—must remain a United Kingdom responsibility.

150. There remains however the question whether responsibility for the court system and its administration should remain with the Government and Parliament, or should be devolved subject to the qualifications noted in the previous paragraph. There are powerful arguments on both sides. The courts are a distinctive part of the Scottish legal heritage, and may therefore seem wholly suitable to be entrusted to the care of Scotland's new Assembly, under Parliament's continuing ultimate sovereignty. The concept of the development of Scots law as a coherent system argues in favour of devolving the courts and the legal system along with the substantive law. It may be difficult, if responsibility is split, to decide the allocation of such border-line topics as court procedure and the law of evidence. On the other hand, it is arguable that the courts are essential elements in the core of constitutional unity of the United Kingdom and in the fabric of law and order; and that since they have to deal with disputes involving both devolved and non-devolved law, they should not be the responsibility of an Assembly which has no functions in the non-devolved fields. The same factors of public policy and national security which are relevant to the police and prosecution functions (paragraph 148 above) point towards maintaining United Kingdom responsibility for the courts and their jurisdiction, administration and procedure.

151. The Government would welcome public comment and discussion before taking a final decision on this question.

Tourism

152. The Scottish administration will be responsible for tourism in Scotland, including the Scottish Tourist Board. Overseas promotion will remain the responsibility of the British Tourist Authority, which will receive funds from the Government for promoting tourism to Scotland as well as to England and Wales. If the Scottish administration want to give the Authority extra funds for specific promotions overseas, or to give work to other agencies, they will be free to do so; but they will not receive extra United Kingdom funds for these purposes.

Other Matters

153. The administration will be responsible also for a wide variety

of other matters such as fire services; betting, gaming and lotteries; fixing public holidays and summer time; the registration of theatrical employers; controlling charitable collections; Sunday observance; shop hours; the functions now carried out by the Registrar General for Scotland such as the registration of births, marriages and deaths and the administration of marriage law (but not the national census—paragraph 165 below); and the licensing of taxis, liquor, and places of entertainment.

154. It will not be possible to decide whether the administration should have a role in relation to broadcasting until the Committee on the Future of Broadcasting, under the chairmanship of Lord Annan, has reported. Technical factors and international obligations will in any event make it essential to keep central control of frequencies and transmitter power.

Nominated Bodies

155. The Scottish administration will be responsible for nominated bodies operating wholly in Scotland on devolved matters unless, exceptionally, it proves necessary in a particular case to set special limitations. This responsibility will include financing, accountability, reporting and appointments (though recommendations for appointments by the Crown will need to be made through the Secretary of State). The administration will inherit all powers under existing legislation affecting those bodies, and will be able to change that legislation if they wish, including abolishing the bodies or creating new ones. If changes are needed in bodies constituted by Royal Charter or Warrant, these bodies will themselves have to apply for the necessary amendments to their constitutions.

156. Bodies operating in Scotland in devolved matters but organised on a United Kingdom or Great Britain basis raise more complicated problems. They will continue initially to operate as they do now; they will have no formal accountability to the Scottish administration and, where they are financed now through Parliament, this will continue. However, by normal consultation and agreement the Government will be able to secure changes in their activities and membership, and executive bodies will be able to act as the agents of the Scottish administration, provided all this can be arranged within the broad scope of the body's general policy, its legal powers and, where appropriate, its continuing primary responsibility to the Government. There will also be provision for the Government, by Order subject to affirmative resolution of Parliament, to make any legal changes which may be needed in the formal structure and powers of a particular body in order to reflect any agreement between them and the Scottish administration, in consultation with the body itself. In the last resort, however, if agreement is not reached on either informal or formal adjustments, the Scottish administration will be free to make quite new arrangements and terminate a particular body's responsibilities in Scotland (unless, exceptionally, the devolution Act contains special provisions about a particular body, like those for the Forestry Commission envisaged in paragraph 142).

157. The staff of a nominated body operating wholly in Scotland in a devolved field who are civil servants will be treated like other civil servants

in the devolved fields; they will continue to belong to a unified United Kingdom service. Any consultations between the administration and the Government about setting up a separate Scottish civil service (paragraph 84 above) would include the future of civil servants serving with nominated bodies. The Scottish administration will inherit whatever responsibilities the Government now have in relation to staff who are not civil servants.

158. With nominated bodies operating on a United Kingdom or Great Britain basis (paragraph 156), there will be no change in responsibility for staff matters.

159. Appendix E lists nominated bodies to which the arrangements in paragraphs 155-158 above are expected to apply.

General Standards
160. There are a number of matters in which common rules and standards are important, either for safety or to maintain a fair and consistent framework for industry and commerce everywhere. These cover the regulation or statutory standards of marketing, composition, labelling and performance of commonly traded articles or goods, including in particular food (and its handling), medicines, drugs, animal feedingstuffs and pesticides; construction standards for vehicles; and safety standards for fuel-burning appliances, for the use of gas, and for articles used in the home such as inflammable textiles. They also include trades unions, industrial relations and the rights of employees; consumer credit; export credit; competition policy; fair trading; insurance; patents, trade marks, designs and copyright; weights and measures; and shipping and civil aviation. Responsibility for these matters, even where they affect fields otherwise devolved, must in general remain with the Government, though as explained in paragraph 145 above the relationship between the Government's responsibility and the responsibilities to be devolved in the field of Scots private law needs further study.

Pay in the Public Sector
161. The Government must retain in their hands all the means necessary to fight inflation, including the degree of control or influence they now have over public sector pay and related conditions, including pensions. The Scottish administration's powers over pay and conditions in the devolved services cannot therefore be unlimited; their decisions will need to be related to wider considerations of national economic or pay policy. Accordingly, there will be a general requirement in the Act for the administration to take account of any such wider considerations brought specially to their attention by the Government. In addition, in fields where the Government now exercise, in one way or another, general control over pay and conditions of service (as in the health service) the consent of the Secretary of State will be required for any changes. Moreover, the Government expect that where pay in any area of the public services is now settled by national negotiations or arrangements covering the whole of Great Britain these will continue—with appropriate representation for the Scottish administra-

tion—after devolution, whether or not the Secretary of State's consent is required to the outcome.

Regulation of the Professions

162. There are certain occupational groups whose training is controlled by statute, or which have legal powers of self-regulation whereby only people recognised by the group can lawfully claim to be qualified to practise its skills. The question arises how far the Scottish administration should be able to legislate about the regulation of such groups.

163. The Government wish to hear comments from appropriate professional bodies before reaching a definite conclusion; but they provisionally favour devolving power to legislate about the control only of professions which in Scotland will be mainly employed by or under contract to the Scottish administration or bodies subordinate to it; examples would be teachers, the health professions and town planners, but not, say, architects or engineers. The Government also provisionally favour devolving power to legislate about the control of the distinctively Scottish legal profession.

Statistics and Other Information

164. The right to collect relevant statistics and other information goes naturally with responsibility for particular services and the Scottish administration will have this right in the devolved fields. The Government expect that, through consultation, the administration would seek to avoid collection demands overlapping with those of the United Kingdom, and to achieve consistency and compatibility with data from other parts of the United Kingdom.

165. The national population censuses gather important information relevant to both devolved and non-devolved matters. They must therefore remain basically a matter for the Government. The Government would however take into account any views of the Scottish administration in determining the scope and content of census-taking, and would hope to continue to conduct it through the Registrar General for Scotland, whose other functions will come under the Scottish administration.

166. The Government will continue to need information on devolved services, for example on matters where they have to provide consistent United Kingdom data to international organisations. Such information would be supplied normally through consultation and agreement; but to ensure that they remain able to meet their responsibilities there will be a general provision in the Act requiring the Scottish administration to furnish information to the Government on request. The Government for their part would seek to respond helpfully to any needs which the Scottish administration had for information on matters not devolved.

167. The Scottish administration and the Government will be bound to safeguard each other's confidential information, and the law on the pro-

tection of official information will apply in devolved matters as it does now in Government matters. The Assembly could however make new laws if it wished about its own information on devolved matters.

Tribunals and Inquiries

168. Within devolved fields, the Scottish administration will inherit any existing statutory powers relating to the establishment or constitution of tribunals and inquiries. They will be able also, if they wish, to change these inherited powers, to set up new tribunals and to make rules of procedure. The Council on Tribunals and its Scottish Committee, which cover matters that will not be devolved as well as those that will, will remain a United Kingdom responsibility.

E.   SUMMARY OF THE SCHEME FOR SCOTLAND

169. These proposals will create for Scotland an elected Assembly which across a great range of subjects will take over the work of Parliament; and they will create a Scottish Executive which, in these subjects, will have wide responsibilities now borne by the Government.

170. There are some specific restrictions and some general constitutional safeguards, but in practice formal intervention by the Government should be exceptional. Within the devolved fields—notably local government, extensive law functions, health, social work, education, housing, physical planning, the environment, roads and traffic, crofting, most aspects of forestry and many aspects of transport—the Scottish Assembly will pass laws and the Scottish Executive will control administration. Organisation and policies in these fields will be a matter for them. To finance what they want to do they will have a block grant from United Kingdom taxation which they can allocate as they wish. They will be able, if they choose, to levy a surcharge on local government revenue.

171. Scottish Ministers—the Secretary of State for Scotland and the Lord Advocate—will continue to have a major role, as Part V explains. In broad terms however control of the great bulk of public services which affect the people of Scotland will be in the hands of the new Scottish institutions.

PART IV: WALES

A. THE BACKGROUND TO DEVOLUTION IN WALES

172. Wales has been politically united with England for much longer than has Scotland, and has been more closely associated in matters of law and administration. Nevertheless, the distinctive traditions and needs of Wales have led to increasing pressure for separate governmental arrangements. More and more government work has been moved to Wales, and more and more bodies set up to deal with Welsh problems. In 1951 the office of Minister for Welsh Affairs was created and allocated to the Home Secretary alongside his other duties; and in 1964 the Government appointed the first Secretary of State for Wales. The work of his department, the Welsh Office, now covers such matters as housing and local government, some industrial development functions, town and country planning, highways, health, personal social services, and primary and secondary education; and he shares responsibility for agricultural policy and its execution. The Secretary of State also has a general role of keeping in touch with government work in Wales that is not his executive responsibility, and representing Wales's interests. This is particularly important in the economic field.

173. The presence of the Secretary of State in the Cabinet and Welsh Office representation on interdepartmental committees has brought great advantages to Wales These advantages must not be lost. The Secretary of State will carry out many important functions. But a Welsh Assembly is needed to administer a wide range of other major matters, so as to make government in Wales more open and more directly accountable to the Welsh people, and to preserve and foster the rich national heritage of the Principality.

174. Plans for the Welsh Assembly represent a major advance from the present position. That position is however not the same as in Scotland. There is no separate legal system and therefore no general problem about distinctive legislation needed for Wales. Moreover, the Government's consultations suggest that whereas public opinion in Scotland favours a legislative assembly, the situation in Wales is different. The desire is for better democratic control over the government already carried out in Wales, particularly by non-elected bodies.

175. The Government have therefore decided in favour of a Welsh Assembly with very substantial policy-making and executive powers and wide responsibility for democratic oversight. The Government believe that such a body will meet the needs and aspirations of the great majority of the people of Wales.

176. The description of the scheme in the following paragraphs is self-contained. For brevity however where features are essentially the

same as those for Scotland they are generally set out in factual terms without repetition of all the reasons set out earlier in this White Paper. Cross references are given where appropriate.

B. CONSTITUTIONAL ARRANGEMENTS

The Welsh Assembly*

177. There will be a single-chamber Welsh Assembly, initially with 72 members—two for each of the 36 Parliamentary constituencies in Wales. At the first election each elector will be able to vote for two candidates, and in each Parliamentary constituency the two with most votes will become Assembly Members. For later elections the Boundary Commission for Wales will divide Parliamentary constituencies as necessary into single-member Assembly constituencies. Each Parliamentary constituency will be allotted one, two or three Assembly seats, according to a formula based on the average size of Parliamentary electorates in Wales. The formula will be this: —

a.	Parliamentary constituency whose electorate is less than 75% of the average electorate	1 Assembly constituency
b.	Parliamentary constituency whose electorate is not less than 75% and not more than 125% of the average electorate	2 Assembly constituencies
c.	Parliamentary constituency whose electorate is more than 125% of the average electorate	3 Assembly constituencies

On present electorates, this system would give an Assembly of about 75 members. The formula will be re-applied, and any necessary re-division made, whenever Parliamentary seats are redistributed. The divisions into Assembly constituencies will be embodied in draft Orders in Council laid before Parliament by the Secretary of State.

178. Everyone entitled to vote in Parliamentary elections, and also peers, will be able to vote in Assembly elections; but no one will have a vote in more than one constituency. The Secretary of State will be responsible for general oversight of Assembly elections and for making rules for them on election expenses and the like.

179. The Assembly will be elected for a normal fixed term of four years, but the Secretary of State will have power to make minor adjustments either way to give a convenient election day.

180. The time, place and other arrangements for the first meeting will be determined by the Secretary of State. Thereafter these matters will be for the Assembly itself to decide.

---

*See also paragraphs 32-42.

181.   Matters affecting Assembly membership, such as the rules about qualification, disqualification, expulsion and resignation, will be dealt with in the Act, as will the special safeguards which Members will need to do their job effectively, such as protection against actions for defamation. Membership of the Assembly will not be barred to Members of the House of Commons or the House of Lords. Practical considerations will often prevent them from standing for election to the Assembly, but it does not seem right that they should be excluded by statute. Qualification and disqualification are dealt with in more detail in Appendix A.

182.   Every candidate elected to the Assembly will have to swear or affirm allegiance to the Crown before taking his seat.

183.   The pay and allowances of Assembly Members will be determined initially by the Secretary of State and thereafter by the Assembly itself.

184.   The Secretary of State will make interim Standing Orders to get the Assembly started, but thereafter it will make its own, subject to any requirements in the Act—for example on the use of committees (paragraphs 188-195 below).

185.   The Assembly will elect from among its members a presiding officer, like the Speaker in the House of Commons.

186.   The Secretary of State will not be an *ex officio* member of the Assembly. But the Assembly and the Secretary of State could arrange by agreement for him to attend and address meetings from time to time.

187.   The use of the Welsh language in Assembly proceedings and working documents will be for the Assembly itself to decide.

Executive Powers and Committees of the Welsh Assembly

188.   Executive powers in the devolved matters will be vested in the Assembly as a corporate body (and a Crown body). This means that there will not be a sharp distinction between an Executive sponsoring policies and an Assembly discussing and questioning these policies. Instead all policy discussion and decision making will rest with the Assembly itself. Most of its work however will be carried out through standing committees set up to deal with particular devolved subjects, like health and education. The Assembly's powers will be exercised (like the Secretary of State's now) in a variety of ways—political or administrative decision, the issuing of circulars, resolutions of the Assembly or committees, and delegated legislation.

189.   This system, which is well suited to a body which will not have to deal with primary legislation, will allow wide democratic participation in making decisions, since all Members will have a positive role. The detailed pattern will to a great extent be for the Assembly itself to decide, but the Act will lay down the general framework.

190. The Act will empower the Assembly to delegate its functions to the committees. The Assembly will be required to set up committees to cover all the main devolved subjects, and to ensure that representation on the committees is broadly based, so as to reflect the political balance in the Assembly.

191. Each subject committee will have a chairman, to conduct the business impartially; there will also be a leader (to be known as the Executive Member), who will take the main initiative on policy and administration and will be the main link with the officials working on the committee's particular subject. A committee will be able to delegate powers to sub-committees or to the Executive Member.

192. The committee chairmen and the Executive Members will be appointed by the Assembly.

193. There will be a central co-ordinating committee (to be known as the Executive Committee) to oversee general policy and the allocation of resources. This will provide a body of manageable size to draw business together, to ensure that cohesive proposals are presented to the Assembly and to act for the Assembly as a whole on major issues affecting several subjects, including discussion with the Government on the size of the block grant.

194. The Executive Committee will comprise all the Executive Members from the major subject committees plus any other members (not exceeding a quarter of the total) specially appointed by the Assembly. The Assembly will also appoint the chairman, to be known as the Chief Executive. There will be no formal limits on the powers of the Executive Committee; but its main purpose will be to settle the allocation of resources between the services administered by the subject committees, and to see that policies are consistent.

195. The control of officials and documents will be formally vested in the Assembly, which will have, as a body, the formal right of full access to departmental papers and officials. However, it would obviously not be consistent with practical government for every Assembly Member to be able to demand the attendance of any official or insist on seeing any document. The Assembly will therefore be empowered to confer right of access only on committees acting in their particular fields of responsibility or, through those committees, on Executive Members or sub-committees similarly acting. Individual Assembly Members will have no general right of access.

Legislation for Wales
196. Parliament will continue to legislate for Wales in the devolved subjects as well as in others. The Welsh Assembly will therefore work within the limits of Westminster Acts. But in controlling the devolved services it will take over whatever powers those Acts confer on central government, including the power to make delegated legislation.

197. This division of responsibility for primary legislation and for execution presents some problems. The formal position is quite clear: the Assembly

will in general be able to do anything in relation to devolved matters that does not require new primary legislation. This means that its powers will vary from service to service, depending on how far primary legislation lays down detailed requirements. In some subjects Westminster Acts are in fairly general terms, leaving plenty of scope for discretion in day-to-day administration; in others they are drawn more tightly. So the degree of freedom which the Assembly will enjoy at the start of its life will to some extent be uneven.

198. As the work of the Assembly develops, new factors will come into play. The Assembly will take a close interest in proposed legislation affecting Wales. It will debate such documents as White Papers and Green Papers outlining the Government's plans for legislation. Its officials will be consulted by their Government counterparts as appropriate when new legislation affecting devolved matters is being prepared. The Assembly will be able to debate Bills as they are published. It will no doubt make representations to the Secretary of State for Wales and to others, such as Welsh Members of Parliament and Government Departments, suggesting how Bills might be improved to fit Welsh needs. It may sometimes take the initiative itself and press for new Westminster legislation. In time Parliament might wish to give the Assembly greater discretion, by passing legislation which would lay down only broad guidelines, leaving the Assembly to fill in the rest.

199. None of this can be exactly planned. Since Parliament cannot bind its successors, there can be no commitment for the future to alter Bills to suit the Welsh Assembly, to introduce legislation for Wales different from that for England, or to implement any concept of "framework" legislation. The pattern must evolve naturally.

200. In the passage of private Bills affecting devolved matters in Wales the Assembly could be given a role similar to that of a Government Department. It would then be able to submit reports for the consideration of any Parliamentary Committee enquiring into the provisions of a Private Bill.

Delegated Legislation

201. In devolved matters the Welsh Assembly will have general responsibility for framing and passing delegated legislation under powers conferred by existing or future Acts of Parliament. There may be some exceptions, but they will be few. In general, the Welsh Assembly will deal with all classes of delegated legisation.

202. Where an Act applying to a devolved field lays down, in order to control expenditure, that delegated legislation shall be made jointly by two or more Ministers or with the consent of the Treasury or the Civil Service Department, the power to make instruments will pass simply to the Assembly. Where an Act confers a power exercisable by Order in Council, that power will become exercisable by Order of the Assembly.

203. The general procedures for making and controlling delegated legislation will need some adaptation to the Welsh situation, where there

40

will not be a separate Assembly and Executive. At present a subordinate instrument is prepared in the appropriate Department, is made by the Minister or Ministers concerned and undergoes any necessary Parliamentary procedure and scrutiny. After devolution all these stages will take place within the Welsh Assembly.

204. All delegated legislation which at Westminster would be subject to the affirmative or negative resolution procedure will require a resolution by the Welsh Assembly in plenary session. Some provision will be needed to enable subject committees to act, and report back later to the full Assembly, in specially urgent cases. The committees will in any case play an important part in framing statutory instruments and considering their merits.

205. Some equivalent is required also to Westminster's Joint Committee on Statutory Instruments. The Assembly will therefore be required to set up, for the general scrutiny of secondary legislation, a committee broadly representative of the Assembly as a whole and not including any member of the Executive Committee. The committee will thus be as independent as possible of those primarily responsible for promoting the statutory instruments which it will examine.

206. At present local authorities, certain statutory undertakings like nationalised industries and a few other bodies like the National Trust have a right to petition Parliament against some Orders which affect them. After devolution petitions against Assembly Orders would have to go to the Assembly itself. The Assembly might in theory appear to be acting as judge in its own cause; but to make Parliament or the Secretary of State for Wales the judge would be inconsistent with genuine devolution. Whatever arrangements the Assembly sets up for hearing such petitions will be expected to provide the greatest possible impartiality.

United Kingdom Reserve Powers*

207. The Government have no intention of monitoring everything the Welsh Assembly does. Nevertheless, the Government must have power to step in where necessary, either because matters not devolved—such as defence—are being prejudiced, or for wider reasons of their ultimate responsibility for all the people of the United Kingdom.

208. The Government will have open to them three methods of intervention, for use either separately or in combination: —

 a. for actions in prospect, whether involving a proposed subordinate instrument or some other proposed executive act, they will be able to issue a direction prohibiting the action or requiring a particular course of action (including the reversal of a previous action), subject to an affirmative resolution of Parliament within a specified period;

*See also paragraphs 71-75.

b. for subordinate instruments already made, they will be able to make an annulment Order following an affirmative resolution of Parliament. In case of urgency the Order can be made without asking Parliament first, but subject to affirmative resolution within a specified period;

c. for other actions already taken, or for omissions, the Government will be able, if the Welsh Assembly declines to put the matter right, to resume responsibility for the devolved subject in question to the minimum extent necessary—for the required place, task or period—with power to require and direct the use of the staff and facilities of the Assembly for the purpose. They will do this by Order, subject to affirmative resolution of Parliament. The powers which the Government will be able to take by such an Order will be any powers available within statute law applying to Wales, though any requirement for Assembly approval will be suspended.

209. These general procedures for intervening in the business of the Assembly are not intended for frequent use. They will be there in the background as reserve powers; and they permit wider devolution than would otherwise be possible. Their use will require the specific agreement of Parliament.

210. All this is about circumstances in which the Government need to intervene on grounds of policy as distinct from law. The legality of the Assembly's actions will be open to challenge in the courts just like that of the Government's own actions.

The Civil Service in Wales

211. The Welsh Office itself will continue to exercise major functions in Wales, and it will also have an important linking role between the Government and the Assembly, particularly in relation to primary legislation. But policymaking and administration in devolved fields now the responsibility of the Welsh Office will be taken over by the Assembly; and the Assembly will therefore need substantial numbers of staff.

212. The Assembly will be a Crown body. Its officials will therefore be civil servants. The question arises whether they should form a separate Welsh civil service, or should be part of the United Kingdom civil service.

213. The Kilbrandon Commission thought that there would have to be a separate civil service, on the grounds that a devolved administration would wish to choose its own senior officials, might not be content for general personnel matters to be handled by a Government Department, and would want to be able to rely on the undivided loyalty of their officials dealing with the Government, for example on the block grant.

214. There are however strong arguments for maintaining a unified service. It would help the consultation and co-operation on which the success of devolution will heavily depend. Present experience does not

42

suggest that with a single service there need be divided loyalty; civil servants by tradition give wholehearted service to whichever Ministers are in charge of their Departments. We cannot assume that all staff will wish to transfer to a service entirely separate from that to which they were recruited, where the work, conditions and prospects might become substantially different.

215. Other factors must be taken into account. A separate service would need more staff (for example to handle personnel matters now dealt with centrally). A unified service would enable the Assembly to draw its officials more easily from a wide pool of talent and experience. The wishes of the Assembly itself will be important, and these cannot be known until it is in being. Finally, even if a separate Welsh service were desirable it could not be set up in time for the start of the Assembly's work; it is an option only for the longer term.

216. The Government believe that it will be in the best interests of all to keep a unified United Kingdom civil service. Any change would be a matter for discussion with the Welsh Assembly; staff representatives would be consulted at all stages. It would be essential to maintain the traditional independence of the recruitment system.

217. Numbers and costs of staff are dealt with in Part VI.

Complaints Machinery

218. Complaints against Government Departments can be investigated by the Parliamentary Commissioner for Administration, the "Ombudsman". Corresponding arrangements for the devolved subjects in Wales will need to be laid down in the Act. The details are outlined in Appendix B. The basic system will remain a matter for Parliament; but the new Welsh Commissioner will report to the Assembly.

European Community and other International Aspects*

219. The Government must remain responsible for all international relations, including those concerned with our membership of the European Community. There can therefore be no question of seeking for the Welsh Assembly any right of formal access to Community or other international bodies. Nevertheless, both in Community and in other contexts international business touches increasingly on matters which will be devolved to the Assembly. The views of the Assembly must be taken into account. Arrangements will therefore be developed for consultation between Members and officials of the Assembly and the Government. These might operate most effectively through the Secretary of State for Wales and through the particular Ministers representing the United Kingdom in Brussels or elsewhere.

220. It is necessary to ensure that any relevant international obligations are properly observed in the devolved fields in Wales. Breach of international

*See also paragraphs 87-92.

obligation will be avoided in the normal way through the close consultation which the Government intend to maintain with the Welsh Assembly. If, exceptionally, this does not work for any reason, and the Assembly takes some action contrary to the United Kingdom's international obligations, the Government will be able to use their reserve powers for dealing with matters unacceptable on policy grounds. These powers have been explained in paragraph 208 above. The use of reserve powers in these cases will not however require the approval of Parliament.

221. Positive action is sometimes needed to fulfil new European Community or other obligations. The Government will keep formal responsibility for all matters relating to international obligations, even when these matters arise in fields otherwise devolved; but the Government will be able at their discretion to delegate to the Welsh Assembly, by Order, the job of taking any necessary action (other than primary legislation) to implement the obligation. The power will be a flexible one, which can be used to delegate action either on a particular item, such as an individual European Community directive, or on a general area of business. The Government envisage that in practice it might well become the normal course to delegate implementation by agreement to the Assembly. The devolution Act will add the Assembly to the category of those who can be designated as implementing authorities under the European Communities Act 1972.

C. FINANCIAL ARRANGEMENTS*

222. Paragraphs 94-100 above explain the basic concepts for the financial arrangements underpinning devolution. These concepts are the same for Wales as for Scotland. Paragraphs 223-232 below set out their detailed application to Wales.

The Block Grant

223. Central governmental finance for the devolved services will be provided essentially by block grant voted by Parliament. The Assembly will have the fullest possible freedom to decide how the money should be spent—how much, for example, should go on roads, houses, schools and hospitals, and where in Wales it should be spent. This is a major economic as well as social power, and will give the Assembly a powerful new instrument for shaping developments over a wide range of services. In 1974-75 public expenditure on the services proposed for devolution was more than £850 million with a further sum of £60 million met by local authorities as loan charges. Had the proposed financial arrangements been in operation this would have involved a block grant of about £650 million, local authority taxation of £90 million and borrowing of more than £150 million. Expenditure on the devolved services would have come to more than half of total identifiable public expenditure in Wales.

---

*See also paragraphs 93-113.

44

224. The Government's decision on the total amount for all the devolved services will not be a matter of simply imposing an arbitrary figure; it will be the outcome of a close and thorough process of discussion each year with the Assembly. Appendix C outlines how this might run in a typical year.

225. The Assembly will base its proposals on its view of Welsh needs in the devolved fields. But the Government must take account also of other needs, both elsewhere in the United Kingdom and in non-devolved fields within Wales. All these needs must then be related to what the United Kingdom can afford for public expenditure against other claims, including the balance of payments, private investment and private consumption, as well as the needs of public industries such as coal and steel which will continue to be very important to Wales.

226. With understanding on both sides agreement should usually be reached on a total accepted as fair both to Wales and to the rest of the United Kingdom. If agreement is not reached the matter will have to be settled by the Government, answerable to Parliament. Parliament, with its Welsh Members alongside those from all other parts of the United Kingdom, will vote the amount for the devolved services, and settle the statutory limits on the Assembly's short-term borrowing and on issues to the Welsh Loans Fund.

Taxation
227. Welsh taxpayers will continue to pay United Kingdom taxes at United Kingdom rates, and these payments will contribute to the central pool of national resources from which the block grant and other national expenditure will be financed according to needs.

228. Local authorities, who will run many of the devolved services, can settle their own levels of taxation, so that there will be some flexibility in the total amount available for the services in Wales. The Assembly will decide both how much of the block grant should be distributed to local government and how to allocate it among individual authorities. In calculating the block grant the Government will in general assume that Welsh local authorities will receive, in relation to their expenditure needs and their taxable resources, provision comparable with that for local authorities in England; whether they in fact levy more or less local tax, and are assigned more or less subsidy from the block grant, will be a matter to be settled in Wales.

229. The Assembly will have an optional power to make a surcharge on local authority taxation; but it will not have to use this unless it runs into deficit or deliberately aims for a higher level of expenditure, for example to meet some particular Welsh priority for which it judges people would be willing to accept higher burdens.

Other Sources of Finance

230. Capital expenditure by local authorities and by other public bodies in devolved fields will continue to be financed by borrowing. Local authorities will continue to have access to the Public Works Loan Board. Other public bodies will have access to a new Welsh Loans Fund for longer-term borrowing, financed from the National Loans Fund and controlled by the Assembly. The main condition on its use will be that on-lending should not be at a lower rate of interest than the corresponding loan from the National Loans Fund. The only long-term borrowing transactions controlled individually by the Government will be those involving foreign currency or overseas sources. However, the Government will also control both the total amount of long-term borrowing and, within this, the total of borrowing from official sources by local authorities and public corporations.

Financial Control and Audit

231. The Act will lay down certain basic features to ensure that there is a sound system for authorising expenditure and reporting on the accounts. In addition to the Welsh Loans Fund, there will be Welsh counterparts of the Consolidated Fund, the Comptroller and Auditor General and the Public Accounts Committee (whose membership will be substantially separate from that of the Executive Committee). The Assembly will have power to appropriate funds to individual services by Assembly Order, corresponding to Appropriation Acts at Westminster.

232. Responsibility for controlling issues from the Welsh Funds and for supervising the arrangements for monitoring and audit will rest squarely with Welsh bodies. Reports by the Welsh Comptroller and Auditor General will go to the Assembly and will be considered by the Welsh Accounts Committee. It will be for the Assembly to decide what action should be taken on the Committee's reports. The Act will however require the publication of these reports, so that expenditure on devolved matters undergoes the same public scrutiny as the corresponding expenditure does now.

D.   THE DEVOLVED SUBJECTS

233. Within the fields to be devolved to the Assembly, and subject only to the framework established by Acts of Parliament, the Welsh Assembly will have full policy-making and executive powers of the kind now vested in Ministers. Provided that their actions are not inconsistent with the statutory framework, they will be able to develop their own distinctive policies and approaches, and to develop new tasks if they wish.

234. This is a concept of wide authority and freedom, and it will be applied to a great range of subjects, as paragraphs 236-273 explain. Appendix D gives a tabular summary.

235. The responsibilities to be transferred on devolution in the various fields will be those which the Government now carry. The proposals do not entail any removal of current tasks or powers from local government.

Local Government

236. Responsibility for central government supervision of most aspects of local government in Wales will be devolved. The administration will oversee the work of local authorities in devolved matters. It will allocate rate support grant to them, control their capital investment in the devolved fields and be responsible for the application of the local taxation system. The devolution Act will make no change in the structure of local government in Wales.

237. Local government administrative and electoral areas and boundaries will remain the responsibility of the Secretary of State, advised by the Local Government Boundary Commission for Wales. The Assembly will not of course be responsible for any functions which Welsh local authorities continue to carry out in matters not devolved; the responsibilities of central and local government in these matters will remain unchanged.

Health*

238. The Assembly will be responsible for health matters in Wales, including the National Health Service. It will be free to settle arrangements and priorities for the provision of health care, including the resources to be allocated, and to develop its own policies on such matters as family planning, private practice and the control of nursing homes. In this as in other fields (see paragraph 267 below) certain general United Kingdom standards will however continue to apply—for example in relation to medicines and drugs.

Personal Social Services†

239. The Assembly will be responsible for such social services as the care of children, the elderly, the handicapped and others in need of special care and protection. It will be able to supervise private provision in these fields, and make grants to voluntary bodies. It will not however be responsible for the probation service.

Social Security‡

240. The social security system and the war pensions scheme will remain on a United Kingdom basis.

241. Some problems arise over schemes for rent and rate rebates, rent allowances, and the minimum charges and personal allowances for those living in local authority homes. The Government's approval will be required for any changes in such schemes which would affect wholly or mainly people receiving supplementary benefits, or people who would receive them if the changes were made. It is a more open question whether, because of the complexity of the interaction with social security generally, it would be better not to devolve powers relating to such schemes at all. The Government would welcome comments from bodies working in this field.

---

*See also paragraph 122.
†See also paragraph 123.
‡See also paragraphs 124-125.

Education, Science and the Arts*

242. The Assembly will be responsible for all educational and cultural matters (including the welfare of the Welsh language) other than those noted in paragraph 243 below. It will control the schools system in Wales, and it will be able to determine the structure of the maintained sector and policy of private schools and nursery education. It will be responsible for youth and community services, and for all further and higher education except the universities. However, since England and Wales operate virtually as a unit in the supply of teachers, the Assembly will be required to conform with guidance from the Government on the total output of teachers in Wales.

243. Responsibility will not be devolved for the Research Councils or the Nature Conservancy Council; for the universities; for national policy on mandatory awards to students on higher education courses (though the Assembly will be responsible for policy on discretionary awards); and for post-graduate awards.

244. The Assembly will be responsible for the arts (except the export control of works of art) and for national and local libraries, museums and galleries.

Housing†

245. The Assembly will be responsible for all aspects of housing, except that the Government will remain responsible for housing finance in the private sector (building society mortgages and the like) and will also keep a reserve power to prevent or restrict increases in public and private sector rents where general economic and counter-inflationary policy makes this necessary. These limited qualifications apart, the Assembly will be able to have its own policies, for both the public and the private sectors, on the provision and upkeep of accommodation, the control of rents, subsidies to local authorities and housing associations, renovation, building standards and slum clearance.

Physical Planning and the Environment‡

246. The Assembly will be generally responsible for physical planning and the environment. It will deal with the various aspects of land use—how to manage its development and control, how to co-ordinate land use planning with (for example) transport planning, and how to provide the general infrastructure needed for the prosperity of Wales. It will deal with the general improvement of the environment; the rehabilitation of derelict land; new towns; and the protection of countryside amenity and landscape.

---

*See also paragraphs 126-130.
†See also paragraph 131.
‡See also paragraphs 132-134.

247. The Assembly will have substantial supervisory powers under the new community land legislation, and will appoint the members of the Land Authority for Wales.

248. The devolution of planning powers will be subject to a continuing right—which should not need to be used often—for the Government to "call in" any particular planning issue for their decision if the general United Kingdom interest is affected, for example on non-devolved matters like defence. The Government will probably also need to keep the right to settle any disputes over compulsory purchase affecting such matters.

249. The Assembly will be responsible for sport and recreation, parks and open spaces, national parks, ancient monuments and historic buildings, public and civic amenities, and a variety of other matters like refuse collection and disposal, cemeteries, markets, fairs and allotments. It will be responsible also for dealing with natural emergencies (though any use of the armed forces to help in these must remain a matter for the Government). It will be responsible for protecting the environment, including preventing nuisances, atmospheric pollution and noise, except that their powers will not extend to aircraft, motor vehicles and ships.

Roads and Transport*

250. The Assembly will be responsible for a wide range of matters in the transport field. These will include the planning, construction and standards of roads; the application of traffic rules (except on motorways, where uniformity throughout Great Britain is important for safety); bilingual road signs; road safety publicity; local transport planning; road service licensing, including appointing Traffic Commissioners and deciding appeals arising from their decisions; powers to subsidise bus and railway passenger services, to be exercised concurrently with similar local authority powers; inland waterways; examining and paying claims for new bus grants; operating the current powers to pay fuel duty rebate to bus operators; and the supervision of local authority airports.

Development and Industry†

251. There will be no change in the powers of the Welsh Development Agency. Its environmental and factory building functions will be fully devolved, except that the terms of disposal of factories will remain under Government control. The other industrial functions of the Agency will remain with the Government. Half the members of the Board of the Agency will be appointed by the Assembly, which will also be consulted before the Secretary of State appoints the Chairman.

252. There can be no question of breaking up the main nationalised industries or splitting responsibility for them. The Government envisage

---

*See also paragraphs 135-137.
†See also paragraphs 138-141.

however that there should be informal contacts between them and the Assembly on matters of joint interest, and that they should include in their reports information on recent developments and future plans for Wales. The Assembly will be able to discuss these reports, and to make representations to the industries or to Ministers.

253. Government Departments operating on a central basis will keep their present statutory functions for industry and commerce; but they will consult the Office of the Secretary of State or the Assembly on matters of common concern.

Natural Resources*

254. The Assembly will be responsible for freshwater fisheries, for management of the agricultural estates now vested in the Secretary of State for Wales, and also for forestry functions (except fiscal, regulatory and international aspects). The Forestry Commission will remain as the instrument for carrying out Welsh policies, for which it will be financed by and accountable to the Assembly.

Water in Wales

255. Decisions taken about water services in Wales can radically affect water supplies in extensive and heavily populated areas of England. In order to match river basins the area of the Welsh National Water Development Authority has to include parts of England and that of the Severn-Trent Regional Water Authority to include parts of Wales. The Government envisage that both authorities should remain in being within their present boundaries and should be responsible to the Welsh Assembly for their operations in Wales and to the Government for their operations in England. Substantial water development and policy changes anywhere in Wales will be subject to the Assembly's agreement. Unresolved cross-border disputes would have to be referred to the Government. The Assembly will provide or nominate the majority of the members of the WNWDA and some members of the STRWA, and will be responsible for water recreation and amenity planning throughout Wales.

256. The Government are currently conducting a general review of the water industry in England and Wales. The details of the arrangements described above may need to be altered in the light of that review.

Tourism

257. The Assembly will be responsible for tourism in Wales, including the Wales Tourist Board. Overseas promotion will remain the responsibility of the British Tourist Authority, which will receive funds from the Government for promoting tourism to Wales as well as to England and Scotland. If the Assembly wants to give the Authority extra funds for specific

---

*See also paragraphs 142-143.

promotions overseas, or to give work to other agencies, it will be free to do so; but it will not receive extra United Kingdom funds for these purposes.

Other Matters

258.   The Assembly will be responsible also (to the extent that there are current governmental functions conferred by primary legislation) for a wide variety of other matters such as fire services; betting, gaming and lotteries; public holidays and summer time; the registration of theatrical employers; controlling charitable collections; Sunday observance; shop hours; the registration of births, marriages and deaths; and the licensing of taxis, liquor and places of entertainment.

259.   It will not be possible to decide whether the Assembly should have a role in relation to broadcasting until the Committee on the Future of Broadcasting, under the chairmanship of Lord Annan, has reported. Technical factors and international obligations will in any event make it impossible to devolve responsibility for allocating frequencies and controlling transmitter power.

Nominated Bodies

260.   The Government attach particular importance to giving the Assembly the maximum role possible in the democratic supervision of nominated bodies now operating in the fields to be devolved. The following paragraphs set out the arrangements which the Government propose for the future treatment of existing bodies.

261.   The Assembly will be responsible for nominated bodies operating wholly in Wales on devolved matters unless, exceptionally, it proves necessary in a particular case to set special limitations. This responsibility will include financing, accountability, reporting and appointments (though recommendations for appointments by the Crown will need to be made through the Secretary of State). The Assembly will inherit all governmental powers under existing legislation affecting those bodies. If changes are needed in bodies constituted by Royal Charter or Warrant, these bodies will themselves have to apply for the necessary amendments to their constitutions.

262.   The Government intend that the Secretary of State should have power, by Order subject to negative resolution procedure at Westminster, to provide that the Welsh Assembly itself should assume the functions of a particular nominated body in Wales. This power would be used in consultation with the Assembly.

263.   Bodies operating in Wales in devolved matters but organised on a United Kingdom, Great Britain or England-and-Wales basis raise complicated problems. The Government at present envisage that these bodies will continue initially to operate as they do now; they will have no formal accountability to the Assembly and, where they are financed now through Parliament, this will continue. However, by normal consultation

51

and agreement the Government will be able to secure changes in their activities and membership, and executive bodies will be able to act as the agents of the Assembly, provided all this can be arranged within the broad scope of the body's general policy, its legal powers and, where appropriate, its continuing primary responsibility to the Government. There will also be provision for the Government, by Order subject to affirmative resolution of Parliament, to make any legal changes which may be needed in the formal structure and powers of a particular body to reflect any agreement between them and the Assembly in consultation with the body itself.

264. The staff of a nominated body operating wholly in Wales in a devolved field who are civil servants will be treated on devolution like other civil servants in the devolved fields; they will continue to belong to a unified United Kingdom service. Any consultations between the administration and the Government about setting up a separate Welsh civil service (paragraph 216 above) would include the future of civil servants serving with nominated bodies. The assembly will inherit whatever responsibilities the Government now have in relation to staff who are not civil servants.

265. With nominated bodies operating on a United Kingdom or Great Britain basis (paragraph 263), there will be no change in responsibility for staff.

266. Appendix F lists nominated bodies to which the arrangements in paragraphs 261-265 are expected to apply.

General Standards*
267. There are a number of matters in which common rules and standards are essential and for which responsibility must therefore remain with the Government. These cover the regulation or statutory standards of marketing, composition, labelling and performance of commonly traded articles or goods, including in particular food (and its handling), medicines, drugs, animal feedingstuffs and pesticides; construction standards for vehicles; and safety standards for fuel-burning appliances, for the use of gas, and for articles used in the home such as inflammable textiles. They also include trades unions, industrial relations and the rights of employees; export credit; competition policy; fair trading; insurance; patents, trade marks, designs and copyright; weights and measures; and shipping and civil aviation.

Pay in the Public Sector†
268. The Assembly will be required to take account, in determining pay and related conditions (including pensions) in the devolved services, of any wider considerations of national economic or pay policy brought specially to their attention by the Government. In addition, in fields where the Government now exercise, in one way or another, general control

---

*See also paragraph 160.
†See also paragraph 161.

over pay and conditions of service (as in the health service) the consent of the Secretary of State will be required for any changes. Moreover, the Government expect that where pay in any area of the public services is now settled by national negotiations or arrangements, these will continue —with appropriate representation for the Welsh Assembly—after devolution, whether or not the Secretary of State's consent is required to the outcome.

Statistics and Other Information*
269. The right to collect relevant statistics and other information goes naturally with responsibility for particular services, and the Assembly will have this right in the devolved fields.

270. The population census for England and Wales must remain basically a matter for the Government. The Government would however take into account any views of the Assembly in determining the scope and content of census-taking in Wales.

271. To ensure that the Government remain able to meet their retained responsibilities there will be a general provision in the Act requiring the Assembly to furnish information to the Government on request.

272. The Assembly and the Government will be bound to safeguard each other's confidential information, and the law on the protection of official information will apply in devolved matters as it does now in Government matters.

Tribunals and Inquiries†
273. Within devolved fields, the Assembly will inherit any existing powers concerning tribunals and inquiries, and will be able to set up non-statutory inquiries.

E.   SUMMARY OF THE SCHEME FOR WALES

274. The scheme will create an elected Welsh Assembly. While the Assembly will not be able to pass primary legislation, there will be a major devolution of policy-making and executive powers covering a great range of subjects now controlled by the Government. The devolved matters for Wales will become the responsibility of the Assembly, working through specialised committees in which all members can take a constructive part.

275. Mainly through the Secretary of State, the Assembly will be able to influence the shaping of United Kingdom legislation that applies to Wales in the devolved fields; and Welsh Members of Parliament will take part in its scrutiny and passage. Within primary legislation, and subject to

---

*See also paragraphs 164-167.
†See also paragraph 168.

a limited number of specific restrictions and to general constitutional safeguards, the use of which should in practice be exceptional, the Assembly will have wide freedom. These fields will include most aspects of supervising local government, health, social services, education, housing, physical planning, the environment and forestry and many aspects of transport and water. In these devolved fields the Assembly will be able in general to do anything that does not need new primary legislation. To finance the devolved services it will have a block grant from United Kingdom taxation, which it can allocate as it wishes. It will be able, if it chooses, to levy a surcharge on local government taxation.

276. The general effect will be to place under immediate Welsh democratic supervision a wide range of services run in Wales for Wales. This will include bringing under the Assembly's control many of the appointed bodies now operating in Wales.

277. The Secretary of State will continue to have a major role, as Part V explains. In broad terms however control of the great bulk of public services which affect the people of Wales will be in the hands of their Assembly.

PART V: DECENTRALISATION—THE EXECUTIVE ROLE OF SCOTTISH AND WELSH MINISTERS IN THE GOVERNMENT

278. Parts III and IV above have set out the subject fields to be devolved to the Scottish and Welsh administrations. All other matters will be reserved to the Government. The Government have however reviewed the full range of these other matters, and intend to allocate important new responsibilities to the Secretaries of State for Scotland and Wales.

279. Decentralisation is not a substitute for devolution. But where it is necessary for powers to remain with the Government, decentralisation enables decision taking within the framework of collective Ministerial responsibility to be moved to Scotland and Wales. It will also make it possible to have simpler and more effective arrangements for informal consultation with the devolved administrations on matters of common concern.

280. Some of the powers which cannot be devolved are already exercised by the Secretaries of State for Scotland and Wales. The Secretary of State for Scotland will remain responsible for the electricity industry. He will also keep the main agriculture and fisheries functions. These are essential national industries, and to avoid market distortions policies must be determined by the Government. There are also important international and European Community aspects. Devolution is therefore impracticable. Where powers are at present exercised in Scotland by the Secretary of State, but for Wales by the Minister of Agriculture, Fisheries and Food (sometimes jointly with the Secretary of State), those for Wales will be transferred to the Secretary of State alone.

281. The Secretaries of State will keep their responsibilities for economic planning and industrial steering and promotion, as well as powers of selective regional industrial assistance under section 7 of the Industry Act 1972, where they will be able at their discretion to arrange for the Scottish and Welsh Development Agencies to act for them. They will also keep their powers of control over the investment and industrial participation activities of the Development Agencies, though all the other powers of the Agencies will be under the direct control of the Scottish and Welsh administrations. The combination of devolved and reserved functions in the Agencies is reflected by the arrangement whereby the Secretaries of State will appoint half the members of the Boards, and will also appoint the Chairmen after consultation with the administrations. Responsibility for the Highlands and Islands Development Board's activities as a whole will be devolved, but the Board's geographical area will continue to be defined by the Secretary of State for Scotland and he will lay down a system of guidelines and cash limits for their activities in non-devolved fields such as assistance to industry, fishing and agriculture.

282. The main new function which will be transferred both to the Secretary of State for Scotland and to the Secretary of State for Wales will be responsibility for the activities in Scotland and Wales of the Manpower Services Commission, the Training Services Agency and the Employment Service Agency. Within the requirements of a single labour market this transfer will help these bodies to give full emphasis to special local conditions. The Government intend to develop with the Scottish and Welsh administrations informal arrangements for co-ordination between these activities and related ones for which the administrations will be responsible, including further education.

283. The Government have considered decentralising to the Secretaries of State for Scotland and Wales responsibility for some or all of the activities in Scotland and Wales of those nationalised industries which cannot be devolved. These include industries which form part of a closely integrated national and in some cases international network (railways, airways, posts and telecommunications) and others (steel, coal, gas) which serve wide markets and must for efficiency continue to be run on a United Kingdom or Great Britain basis. In these cases (and also with ports, for which the Government will soon be bringing forward nationalisation proposals) transfer to the Secretaries of State of formal responsibilities for a geographical part of the operations would make little sense. The Secretaries of State already share however in Government decisions affecting these industries (including appointments to their associated consumer bodies) in Scotland and Wales, and the importance of this involvement will be enhanced by their new economic functions.

284. Since the Government bear the prime responsibility for protecting the interests of all citizens of the United Kingdom and the security of the nation there are other functions outside the economic field where devolution is not feasible; certain law and functions in Scotland—such as those relating to the police and the prosecution system—are notable examples. Most of these will however continue to be exercised by Scottish Ministers—the Secretary of State or the Lord Advocate.

285. Taken together, the decentralisation proposals will give the Secretaries of State for Scotland and Wales an enhanced and very substantial economic role, monitored by Parliament with its full complement of Scottish and Welsh Members. The Secretaries of State and the Lord Advocate will also retain a wide general role, even in matters where it has not been necessary to create formal arrangements, in advising their colleagues in the Government on particular Scottish and Welsh considerations. All this will complement the devolution schemes in ensuring that decisions on a very wide range of Government activity are made in Scotland and Wales, whether by the devolved administrations or by Scottish and Welsh Ministers, and that decisions which have to be made elsewhere take full account of the Scottish and Welsh dimension.

PART VI: COSTS

286. The long-term cost of devolution in manpower and money cannot be calculated exactly. No one can forecast how successful the new administrations will be in providing devolved services economically, or what changes they may choose to make in the organisation and conduct of business. Estimates made now can be based only upon a broad assessment of how the devolved administrations, and the Scottish and Welsh Offices in their new form, are likely to operate when they are first established. Furthermore, the main policy decisions are still recent; there must be continued study of detail, some of which could have cost implications.

287. Devolution must mean some increase in the direct costs of government. There will be entirely new activities, not least the running of the Assemblies themselves; there will be some loss of economies of scale in support services; there will be new and sometimes unavoidably complex divisions of responsibility; and it must be likely that in some of the devolved fields the new administrations will wish to make less use than the Scottish and Welsh Offices do of the specialised expertise of London-based Departments.

288. It would however be quite wrong to suppose that devolution means vast new bureaucracies. In essence, it is not the creation of new administrative machines but the transfer of responsibility for existing ones to new centres of democratic accountability.

289. On provisional estimates made so far, the scheme for Scotland might mean a capital outlay of some £2-3 million (for the conversion of the former Royal High School building in Edinburgh to house the Assembly), extra staff of about 1,000 (including 200 for the Assembly itself) and extra annual running costs of around £10 million.

290. The picture is different in Wales, since there has been less decentralisation; the Welsh Office is far smaller than the Scottish Office. The extra requirement in Wales is therefore both larger (because extra functions will be transferred to the Principality) and more difficult to estimate closely. Broadly however the extra staff might be around 600 initially, rising thereafter to about 1,600 when the Assembly gets into its stride. At the earlier level the extra running costs would be around £5 million, rising at the later stage to around £12 million. Preparing the Temple of Peace and Health in Cardiff (if it can be made available) for the Assembly might mean a capital outlay of £1-2 million.

291. The transfer of responsibilities to the new administrations will affect the tasks of other Government Departments as well as the Scottish and Welsh Offices. It is not yet possible to estimate all the effects, even

broadly, but there ought to be net savings in these other Departments, particularly in relation to Wales.

292.   These last effects apart, the schemes for Scotland and Wales together might mean, in total, capital costs of around £4 million, extra staff building up to some 2,500-3,000 and annual costs building up to around £22 million. Such costs are naturally in themselves unwelcome, especially in current economic circumstances. They must however be seen in perspective; they relate to a major gain in democratic control and accountability for public services which last year cost nearly £2,900 million. Against this background, the Government do not regard them as disproportionately heavy.

PAGE VII: WHAT SCOTTISH AND WELSH DEVOLUTION WILL MEAN FOR THE UNITED KINGDOM

293. The Government's proposals for Scotland and Wales envisage powerful and wide-ranging new systems of democratic control to meet the desire of the Scottish and Welsh people for more direct and effective involvement in the running of their own affairs, recognising their distinctive identities within the wider framework of which they will remain part. The proposals however will rightly evoke interest not in those countries alone, but throughout the United Kingdom. The Government will therefore welcome wide discussion and comment. The essential political and economic unity of the United Kingdom has the corollary that what happens to the part must be of concern to the whole. It is to the benefit of all our citizens, wherever they live, that that unity should be preserved; the Government have taken this as a constant and cardinal principle in devising their proposals. Irrespective of any later plans for England or Northern Ireland, devolution must never be seen as conferring unfair advantages on Scotland and Wales.

294. The Government look forward to public debate on their proposals. These proposals are designed to strike a careful balance—in particular, between the desirability of allowing the maximum local freedom and initiative and the need to safeguard the unity of the United Kingdom; and between maximising local democratic control over the allocation of expenditure on the public services and the continuing responsibility of the Government for managing the economy. Any suggestions for modifying the proposals will also have to pay regard to these considerations if they are to command widespread acceptance.

295. After devolution to Scotland and Wales, each part of the United Kingdom will have a different form of government. There is nothing new about this. Northern Ireland had a separate Parliament from 1920 to 1973, and more recently its own Assembly. Scotland has had its own Minister in the Government for very many years, and a wide range of powers and functions have been decentralised to him. The system in Wales is similar in principle, but newer and less extensive. Arrangements in the English regions are different again, with regional offices of central government backed up by advisory bodies such as the regional economic planning councils.

296. The unity and coherence of British society will not be destroyed. Changes in our democratic machinery will not harm the deep sense of allegiance to the United Kingdom as a whole felt by our peoples; indeed, their success depends upon it. Nothing in the Government's present proposals will weaken the powerful social and cultural influences which help to build unity—highly developed communications; widely-circulating news-

papers; radio and television; and above all a close web of ties in family and friendship throughout the United Kingdom. The peoples of Scotland and Wales will find it welcome that, within a larger unitary state, they will have their own Assemblies, concerned to foster their culture and traditions and to satisfy their needs in the ways they wish. The United Kingdom will still be a single state; the Scottish and Welsh administrations will have no separate authority in international relations. Parliament will remain ultimately sovereign in all matters, whether devolved or not, and will continue to include the present complement of Scottish and Welsh Members.

297. The United Kingdom economy will continue to be managed as one unit, with all contributing through the tax system according to their means and for the benefit of all. It is not the purpose of devolution to give Scotland and Wales more and more while the rest of the United Kingdom gets less and less. The object is rather to give Scotland and Wales more freedom to decide what to do with their fair share—a discretion to improve the use rather than to raise the consumption of resources. The economic position of a country or region will not depend on the tax revenue which it happens to produce at a particular period; vigorous regional policies will continue, with the aim of achieving the fairest possible division of jobs and investment between different areas of the United Kingdom. And the Secretaries of State for Scotland and Wales, alive to the traditions and needs of their countries and charged with both constitutional and economic functions, will help to ensure that relations between the Government and the new administrations are marked by creative co-operation.

298. Any change in the machinery of democratic government must bring new problems in its wake. The Scottish and Welsh Assemblies will no doubt have teething troubles, and there will be a financial price to pay. This however is well worth accepting in order to meet the clear popular demand in Scotland and Wales for bringing nearer home the democratic control of much government activity. The proposals set out in this White Paper are a response to differing needs in the ways best matched to them. This flexibility will give renewed vigour and strength to our unity.

SCOTTISH AND WELSH ASSEMBLIES:
QUALIFICATION AND DISQUALIFICATION FOR MEMBERSHIP

1. The rules on qualification and disqualification for membership of the Assemblies will be the same for both Scotland and Wales.

Qualification for Membership

2. Candidates should be (as for the House of Commons): —

    a. at least 21 years of age; and

    b. a British subject or a citizen of the Republic of Ireland.

Disqualification for Membership

3. The following persons will be disqualified: —

    a. persons who are disqualified for House of Commons member-ship as holding any of the offices set out in section 1 of the House of Commons Disqualification Act 1975, such as judges, civil servants, and members of police forces or of the regular armed services;

    b. persons holding certain other listed offices, including chairman-ship or membership of a wide range of commisions, boards, administrative tribunals, public authorities and undertakings. The general criteria for drawing up the list are described in paragraph 4;

    c. persons under sentence of treason;

    d. persons whose estate has been sequestrated or who have been adjudged bankrupt; and

    e. persons who are guilty of corrupt or illegal practices at elections under Part III of the Representation of the People Act 1949, which will be applied to the Assemblies.

4. The general criteria for drawing up the list of disqualifying offices mentioned in paragraph b. above will be these: —

    a. paid office holders whose functions are confined to Scotland or Wales and who will in future be appointed by the Scottish or Welsh administrations will normally be disqualified from the Assembly of the country in which they perform their functions and generally also from the House of Commons, but not from the other Assembly;

    b. persons who hold paid office in bodies appointed by the United Kingdom Government and who are disqualified from the House of Commons will normally be disqualified from the Scottish or Welsh Assembly if the functions of the body extend to Scotland or Wales respectively, but not otherwise;

    c. unpaid office holders will be disqualified only if the office might make it impossible for its holder to fulfil his Assembly duty satisfactorily or if it is particularly important that the holder of the particular office concerned should be seen to be free from political bias. Where disqualification is regarded as appropriate for these reasons, its territorial application will follow that for paid offices.

5. Members of the United Kingdom Parliament, including peers and peeresses, will not be disqualified. Nor will a member of one Assembly be disqualified from membership of another.

6. No clergy of any denomination will be disqualified from the Assemblies.

7. The proposed rules on disqualification are in substance the same as those for the House of Commons, except in respect of clergy and peers.

Alterations to the Scope of Disqualification

8. There will be two ways of altering the lists of disqualifying offices. One will be primary legislation by Parliament, for example when new public offices are established whose functions extend to Scotland or Wales. The other will be by Order in Council. It will be open to the Assemblies to resolve that the list should be altered, for example in consequence of a new Scottish Assembly Act; and the Government would take note of any such resolution.

Exclusion and Expulsion of Members from the Assemblies

9. An Assembly will be able to exclude for a limited period Members who are obstructing business to an intolerable extent. This will be done under the Assembly's own Standing Orders, as part of the day-to-day conduct of business. In addition, the Act will lay down that failure to attend meetings of the Assembly or its committees for any period of six consecutive months will result in the Member's seat becoming vacant, unless the absence is specifically approved by the Assembly.

Repercussions on Membership of the House of Commons

10. Members of the Assemblies will not be disqualified for membership of the House of Commons. But some office holders under the Assemblies will need to be added to the list of those disqualified from the House of Commons.

COMPLAINTS MACHINERY IN SCOTLAND AND WALES

1. The existing complaints machinery (the "Ombudsman" system) is an important protection for the citizen, and the Government will establish comparable machinery to investigate complaints of maladministration by the Scottish and Welsh administrations in the devolved fields.

2. Scottish and Welsh Assembly Commissioners will be appointed by Her Majesty. Action will be initiated by a complaint to an Assembly Member which will then be passed to the Commissioner; in Wales, where the Assembly will be the executive and can itself be the body complained against, there will be additional provision for the Commissioner to accept a complaint direct from the public where an Assembly Member has declined to pass it on.

3. Subject to exclusions comparable to those applying to the Parliamentary Commissioner, the Scottish Assembly Commissioner will be able to investigate any action taken in the exercise of administrative functions by a department serving the Scottish Executive. The Welsh Assembly Commissioner will have a similar power in relation to action taken by or on behalf of the Welsh Assembly by Members, committees, or officers.

4. The Commissioners will make periodic general reports to the Assemblies. They will also be able to make special reports, for example on cases where the injustice has not been or will not be remedied.

5. The investigation of complaints about the activities of the Scottish and Welsh Offices and other Government Departments will remain the responsibility of the Parliamentary Commissioner.

6. Where a Government Department or one of the devolved administrations is acting as agent for the other, or where a complaint covers both devolved and non-devolved matters, the Government Department's actions will be investigated by the Parliamentary Commissioner and the administration's actions by the appropriate Assembly Commissioner.

7. The complaints machinery for the health service in Scotland and Wales will continue, but with procedural modifications so that the Commissioners report to the devolved administrations. The complaints machinery for local government in Scotland and Wales will continue as at present.

8. Legislative responsibility for all these Commissioners will remain with Parliament. In the longer term, when the Government and the devolved administrations have had some experience of operating after devolution, there may be scope for them, in collaboration, to consider streamlining the present system.

PUBLIC EXPENDITURE AND BLOCK GRANT CONSULTATIONS: AN ILLUSTRATIVE ANNUAL CALENDAR

February

i. Start of new annual public expenditure review cycle. Repricing and updating by officials of figures in the last annual United Kingdom White Paper on public expenditure, which will have covered the financial year about to close and the subsequent four years. Discussion of appropriate basis for extending the horizon forward to include the new fifth year.

May-June

ii. After joint technical appraisal, officials report to the Scottish and Welsh administrations and to the Government on the prospects for expenditure in the new four-year period ahead, including the new fifth year.

June-September

iii. Proposals for modification of the public expenditure projections for future years assessed and discussed at official level. Outstanding issues discussed at Ministerial level with members of the Scottish and Welsh administrations. (At the same time, within the Government, assessment and discussion of the proposals affecting the non-devolved services, including those for which the Secretaries of State for Scotland and Wales will be responsible.)

September-October

iv. Cabinet decisions on expenditure priorities.

December-January

v. Publication in the annual United Kingdom White Paper of outcome of the public expenditure review for the subsequent four financial years, including the levels of provision for devolved services in Scotland and Wales.

vi. Publication by the Scottish and Welsh administrations, if they so wish, of their own proposals for allocating Scottish and Welsh provisions to individual devolved services.

February-March

vii. Publication of Supply Estimates setting out the White Paper decisions for which provision is required in the next financial year. Submission of the Scottish and Welsh block grant Estimate for approval by Parliament. (Allocation of the block grant when approved by Parliament would be a matter for the Scottish and Welsh Assemblies, using their own Assembly procedures for appropriation to individual services.)

Note: Arrangements will be made during the financial year for Supplementary Estimates procedures to vote any appropriate additional finance to the devolved services.

OUTLINE OF SUBJECT FIELDS TO BE DEVOLVED

Notes: a. The references to the main matters are to the functions as they exist now. The Scottish Assembly will be able to legislate to develop new or to modify or abolish existing functions within devolved fields. In Wales the Assembly will be able to act within the framework established by Acts of Parliament.

b. This list should be taken in conjunction with relevant sections of the White Paper, including paragraphs 87-92 and 155-168 (Scotland) and paragraphs 219-221 and 260-273 (Wales), which deal with certain general matters affecting several or all subject fields.

1. Local Government—see paragraphs 119-121 (Scotland) and 236-237 (Wales).

The main devolved matters will be:—

i. the general supervision of local government, including (in Scotland) the allocation among local authorities of functions in devolved fields and local government structure and administrative and electoral areas and boundaries;

ii. the financial arrangements of local government, including the amount and distribution of rate support grant, the approval of capital investment and the detailed application of the local tax system. (Power to legislate on the sources of local taxes and on borrowing will not be devolved.)

2. Health—see paragraphs 122 (Scotland) and 238 (Wales).

The main devolved matters will be:—

i. the structure and operation of the National Health Service;

ii. policy on private practice (including its supervision) and private hospital facilities;

iii. general health matters, such as the prevention and notification of infectious diseases and control of nursing homes;

iv. policy on such matters as abortion and the use of dead bodies and organs;

v. radiological protection.

3. Personal Social Services (in Scotland, Social Work)—see paragraphs 123 (Scotland) and 239 (Wales).

The main devolved matters will be:—

i. care and support of children (including the supervision of children who have been before the courts and, in Scotland, Children's Hearings), the handicapped and the elderly, and other groups in need of special care or support such as drug addicts and alcoholics;

ii. supervision of the standards of private provision in these fields, and grants to voluntary bodies.

4. Education and the Arts—see paragraphs 126-130 (Scotland) and 242-244 (Wales).

The main devolved matters will be:—

i. schools, including organisation, attendance requirements and curricula;

ii. further and higher education, except universities;

iii. certain awards to students;

iv. adult education;

v. youth and community services;

vi. national and local museums and libraries;

vii. the arts.

5. Housing—see paragraphs 125 and 131 (Scotland) and 241 and 245 (Wales).

The main devolved matters will be:—

i. the provision, upkeep and improvement of housing accommodation by private owners and public authorities;

ii. public sector housing finance; subsidies to local authorities and housing associations; and control of rents in the public and private sectors.

6. Physical Planning and the Environment—see paragraphs 132-134 (Scotland) and 246-249 and 255-256 (Wales).

The main devolved matters will be:—

i. land use and development, including protection of countryside amenity and landscape;

ii. most executive aspects of the community land scheme;

iii. environmental improvement, and rehabilitation of derelict land (including all the environmental functions of the Scottish and Welsh Development Agencies);

iv. water, river management, arterial drainage and flooding, sewerage and sewage disposal and water recreation and amenity planning;

v. new towns;

vi. other environmental functions, including

  a. allotments

  b. ancient monuments and historic buildings

  c. buildings: design and construction standards and building regulations

  d. burial and cremation; and provision of mortuaries

  e. commons registration and management (applicable only to Wales)

  f. markets and fairs

  g. national parks (applicable only to Wales)

  h. protection of the environment generally, including the prevention of nuisances and control of noise and pollution of the atmosphere (except in relation to aircraft, motor vehicles and ships)

   i. provision and protection of public and civic amenities

   j. refuse collection and disposal

   k. sport and recreation, including the provision of parks and open spaces.

7. Roads and Transport—see paragraphs 135-137 (Scotland) and 250 (Wales).

The main devolved matters will be:—

   i. roads (including motorways)—planning, construction and standards;

   ii. the local application of rules for the management of road traffic (except on motorways) and, in Wales, the authorisation of bilingual traffic signs;

   iii. road safety publicity;

   iv. road service licensing, the appointment of Traffic Commissioners and appeals from Traffic Commissioners in cases involving services wholly within Scotland or Wales;

   v. local transport planning (including in Wales powers, concurrent with those exercised by local authorities, for the Assembly to subsidise bus and rail passenger services);

   vi. bus and shipping services operated by the Scottish Transport Group;

   vii. payment of new bus grants;

   viii. payment of bus fuel duty rebate;

   ix. subsidies for Scottish internal air and shipping services;

   x. local authority airports (arrangements for devolving other publicly-owned airports in Scotland will be discussed with the Scottish administration);

   xi. inland waterways.

8. Development and Industry—see paragraphs 138-141 (Scotland) and 251-253 (Wales).

The devolved matters will be:—

   i. factory building by the Scottish and Welsh Development Agencies and the Highlands and Islands Development Board, new town corporations and local authorities (subject to Government control of the terms of disposal);

   ii. all other functions of the Highlands and Islands Development Board (subject to retention of the Board and to Government control in certain fields).

9. Natural Resources—see paragraphs 142-143 (Scotland) and 254 (Wales).

The main devolved matters will be:—

   i. forestry functions, except for fiscal, regulatory and international aspects, and subject to retention of the Forestry Commission;

ii. management of the agricultural estates now vested in the Secretaries of State for Scotland and Wales;

iii. smallholdings;

iv. crofting (Scotland only);

v. agricultural landlord/tenant relationships;

vi. improvement of fisheries harbours (Scotland only);

vii. freshwater fisheries.

10. Scottish Law Functions—see paragraphs 144-151.
The main devolved matters will be:—

i. as much of private law as proves, on further study, to be compatible with consistency in matters of wider United Kingdom interest, including the maintenance of a common framework for trade;

ii. the general criminal law (except for offences concerning the security of the state, matters for which uniformity is important— eg explosives, firearms and dangerous drugs and poisons—and matters relating to subject fields which will not be devolved, such as tax and motoring offences;

iii. the treatment of offenders;

iv. executive responsibility for the Scottish Law Commission.

Responsibility for the supreme courts, the sheriff courts, the district courts and related matters needs further consideration.

11. Tourism—see paragraphs 152 (Scotland) and 257 (Wales).
Responsibility for tourism in Scotland and Wales will be devolved, subject to the retention of the British Tourist Authority for overseas promotion.

12. Other Matters—see paragraphs 153-154 (Scotland) and 258-259 (Wales).
The devolved matters will include:—

i. fire services;

ii. miscellaneous regulatory functions: licensing of taxis, liquor and places of entertainment; shop hours;

iii. betting, gaming and lotteries;

iv. the fixing of public holidays and summer time;

v. registration of births, marriages and deaths;

vi. records and archives;

vii. byelaws in devolved fields.

68

SCOTLAND: LIST OF NOMINATED BODIES IN DEVOLVED SUBJECTS

Paragraphs 155-159 of the White Paper refer. Bodies covered by special arrangements described elsewhere in the White Paper, such as the Forestry Commission, the Scottish Development Agency and the Highlands and Islands Development Board, are not listed.)

The bodies listed here are those which operate under Royal Charter or Warrant or under statute. The lists are not intended to be definitive. Bodies formed by administrative arrangements, and statutory bodies to which no appointment has been made by the Government, are excluded.

A. Bodies operating on a United Kingdom or Great Britain basis

Arts Council of Great Britain

Board of Trustees of the Central Bureau for Educational Visits and Exchanges
British Library Board

Central Council for Education and Training in Social Work
Council for Educational Technology
Council for the Education and Training of Health Visitors
Council for National Academic Awards
Council for the Professions Supplementary to Medicine

Fire Service College Board

Gaming Board for Great Britain
General Dental Council
General Medical Council
General Optical Council
General Practice Finance Corporation

Horse Race Betting Levy Board
Horse Race Totalisator Board
Housing Association Registration Advisory Committee
Housing Corporation

National Radiological Protection Board

Pharmaceutical Society of Great Britain

Royal Commission on Environmental Pollution

B. Bodies operating only in Scotland

(This list includes bodies subordinate to or established by bodies operating on a wider basis.)

Advisory Council on Social Work
Ancient Monuments Board for Scotland
Area Nurse Training Committees

Board of Management for Schemes of Pensions for Widows and other Dependants of Teachers in Scotland
Board of Trustees of the Scottish National War Memorial
Building Standards Advisory Committee

Central Midwives Board for Scotland
Children's Panels
Children's Panels Advisory Committees
Clean Air Council for Scotland
Commission for Local Authority Accounts in Scotland
Common Services Agency for the Scottish Health Service
Countryside Commission for Scotland
Crofters' Commission

Fire Services (Scotland) Examinations Board

General Nursing Council for Scotland
General Teaching Council for Scotland
Governing Bodies of Central Institutions

Health Boards
Historic Buildings Council for Scotland

Legal Aid Central Committee
Local Government Boundary Commission for Scotland
Local Review Committees (Prisons and Young Offenders' Institutions)

Mental Welfare Commission for Scotland

National Health Service Tribunal
National Optical Consultative Committee
National Panel of Specialists
New Town Development Corporations
New Town Licensing Planning Committees

Panel for the Independent Schools Tribunal
Parole Board of Scotland

Red Deer Commission
Rent Assessment Panel for Scotland
Rent Tribunals
Royal Commission on the Ancient and Historical Monuments of Scotland
Royal Fine Art Commission for Scotland

Scottish Arts Council
Scottish Central Fire Brigades Advisory Council
Scottish Certificate of Education Examination Board
Scottish Dental Estimates Board
Scottish Health Service Planning Council
Scottish Housing Advisory Committee
Scottish Hospital Endowments Research Trust
Scottish Hospital Trust
Scottish Medical Practices Committee
Scottish National Camps Association
Scottish Records Advisory Committee

70

Scottish River Purification Boards
Scottish Special Housing Association
Scottish Sports Council
Scottish Teachers Salaries Committee
Scottish Tourist Board
Scottish Transport Group
Scottish Valuation Advisory Council
Scottish Water Advisory Committee
State Hospital Management Committee

Trustees, National Galleries of Scotland
Trustees, National Library of Scotland
Trustees, National Museum of Antiquities of Scotland

Visiting Committees, HM Borstal Institutions, HM Detention Centre
Glenochil, HM Young Offenders' Institutions

WALES: LIST OF NOMINATED BODIES IN DEVOLVED SUBJECTS

(Paragraphs 260-266 of the White Paper refer. Bodies covered by speci arrangements described elsewhere in the White Paper, such as the Wel Development Agency and the Forestry Commission, are not listed.)

The bodies listed here are those which operate under Royal Charter Warrant or under statute. The lists are not intended to be definitive. Bodi formed by administrative arrangement, and statutory bodies to which appointment has been made by the Government, are excluded.

A. **Bodies operating on a United Kingdom, Great Britain or England an Wales basis**

Advisory Committee on Rent Rebates and Rent Allowances
Arts Council of Great Britain

Board of Trustees of the Central Bureau for Educational Visits an Exchanges
British Library Board
Building Regulations Advisory Committee
Burnham Committees

Central Council for Education and Training in Social Work
Central Fire Brigades Advisory Council for England and Wales
Central Health Services Council and associated Standing Committee
Central Midwives Board
Clean Air Council
Council for Educational Technology
Council for the Education and Training of Health Visitors
Council for National Academic Awards
Council for the Professions Supplementary to Medicine
Countryside Commission

Dental Estimates Board

Fire Service College Board
Fire Services Central Examinations Board

Gaming Board for Great Britain
General Dental Council
General Medical Council
General Nursing Council for England and Wales
General Optical Council
General Practice Finance Corporation

Horse Race Betting Levy Board
Horse Race Totalisator Board
Housing Association Registration Advisory Committee
Housing Corporation

Medical Practices Committee

National Health Service Tribunal
National Radiological Protection Board
National Water Council

Pharmaceutical Society of Great Britain
Public Health Laboratory Service Board

Royal Commission on Ancient Monuments
Royal Commission on Environmental Pollution

Severn-Trent Water Authority

Welfare Panel of the Appeal Tribunal
Welsh National Water Development Authority

B. Bodies operating only in Wales

(This list includes bodies subordinate to or established by bodies operating on a wider basis.)

Ancient Monuments Board for Wales
Area Health Authorities

Central Advisory Council for Education (Wales)
Community Health Councils
Countryside Commission, Committee for Wales
Court and Council of the National Library of Wales
Court and Council of the National Museum of Wales

Historic Buildings Council for Wales

Library Advisory Council (Wales)
Licensing Planning Committees

National Parks Committees
New Town Development Corporations
New Town Licensed Premises Committees

Rent Assessment Panel for Wales
Rent Tribunals
Royal Commission on Ancient and Historical Monuments (Wales)

Sports Council for Wales

Wales Tourist Board
Welsh Arts Council
Welsh Health Technical Services Organisation
Welsh Medical Committee
Welsh Nurse Training Committee
Welsh Nursing and Midwifery Committee
Welsh Pricing Committee

Printed in England for Her Majesty's Stationery Office by Williams Lea, London
Dd 110924 K160 11/75